Sex Games For Couples

Injecting the Playful and Naughty Mood in Your Relationship Whether You are Married or Dating | Perfect Guide for Couples' Truth or Dare Games

Jenny Love

© **Copyright 2021 by Jenny Love - All rights reserved.**

This document is geared towards providing exact and reliable information in regard to the topic and issue covered.

- From a Declaration of Principles which was accepted and approved equally by a Committee of the American Bar Association and a Committee of Publishers and Associations.

In no way is it legal to reproduce, duplicate, or transmit any part of this document in either electronic means or in printed format. All rights reserved.

The information provided herein is stated to be truthful and consistent, in that any liability, in terms of inattention or otherwise, by any usage or abuse of any policies, processes, or directions contained within is the solitary and utter responsibility of the recipient reader. Under no circumstances will any legal responsibility or blame be held against the publisher for any reparation, damages, or monetary loss due to the information herein, either directly or indirectly.

Respective authors own all copyrights not held by the publisher.

The information herein is offered for informational purposes solely and is universal as so. The presentation of the information is without contract or any type of guarantee assurance.

The trademarks that are used are without any consent, and the publication of the trademark is without permission or backing by the trademark owner. All trademarks and brands within this book are for clarifying purposes only and are owned by the owners themselves, not affiliated with this document.

Table of Contents

Introduction 1

Chapter 1. Why Sex Games Are Important for Your Sexual Life? 5

Chapter 2. How to Introduce Sex Games in Your Bedroom? 11

Chapter 3. Role-Playing Sex Games 17

Chapter 4. Classic Erotic Games 23

Chapter 5. Creative Sex Games 27

Chapter 6. Fantastic Sex Games 31

Chapter 7. Kissing Games 37

Chapter 8. Oral Sex Games 45

Chapter 9. Sex Games with Drinks 51

Chapter 10. Hottest Sex Games 55

Chapter 11. Advanced Sex Games for Adventurous Couples 65

Chapter 12. Sex Toys 71

Chapter 13. Fantasies 85

Chapter 14. Naughty Questions 91

Chapter 15. Quick and Easy Foreplay Games for Couples 97

Chapter 16. Fun Sexy Games for Couples 105

Chapter 17. Truth or Dare" Hot 113

Chapter 18. Never Have I Ever 117

Chapter 19. Where to Get Sexy Ideas 121

Chapter 20. Make Love to the Next Level 127

Chapter 21. Tips to Spice up Your Love Life 133

Chapter 22. 5 Tips to Increase Intimacy 139

Chapter 23. Online Interactive Sex Games 145

Conclusion 149

Introduction

Sex games can be used to explore or enhance existing sexual relationships, although they can also be derided as a copout for couples that are sexually incompatible. The release of the sensual text-based cards against humanity game has helped expand the idea of parties involving sex games. Game night, couples may play a variety of games to choose more intimate and sensual sex games. These are the sex games that can be used to explore or enhance existing sexual relationships, although they can also be derided as a copout for couples that are sexually incompatible.

Among these games are card games that involve sexual acts with partners or group sex play. The game is enjoyed when playing sexual games because the rules are there to be broken. There are a few common types of sex games that people enjoy playing. By attending a game night or simply having the environment and willingness to play certain sex games, couples can explore that potential sexual activity together.

Dirty wife, Master of Broken Things is a new video game that is played on a website that is set up in several cities across England and allows couples to play the Master of Broken Things sex game. There are many couples who choose to play sex games for a few reasons, this includes: The release of the sensual text-based Cards against Humanity game has helped expand the idea of parties involving sex games.

After a long day at work or even a long week, it can get boring. Couples who have been dating longer may be concerned with whether or not their relationship can withstand sex games. Some couples may choose to play sex games for a myriad of good reasons, including: games, couples may be able to explore and enjoy sex games together. It is important to understand that sex games are not a replacement for intimacy. If couples feel that sex games are becoming a central focus of their relationship, they should consider breaking out of those games and explore activities that are more intimate together. To prevent separations, couples should not allow themselves to become too bored.

Setting the mood with sex games is a big part of the experience. There are certain rules that must be followed when playing a sex game to avoid becoming too frustrated. Games are always better when they begin by allowing couples to build up a comfortable and sensual tension to get them into the mind frame for playing. In order to avoid frustration, one should make sure to participate enthusiastically with the method of play. If sex games do not feel right, it is best to break out of them rather than continuing with a game that is not working. Sex games are not the same as men feeling less of a sexual desire. Unwillingness to explore sex games is not the same as a man feeling less of a sexual desire. If couples are not doing anything too sexually adventurous, sex games are not always a replacement for a more intimate or satisfying experience.

Avoiding sex games because couples find it uncomfortable is a good reason for couples to reconsider whether their relationship can handle it. If the ability of a marriage to handle sex games is a concern, couples should always try to foster that desire. If a spouse is unsure or does not feel that he or she can explor potential sex games with their partner, their partner should choose a more predictable method of performing the sex act.

People who participate in sex games are choosing to play a game. Sex games do not imply that a couple wants to have a sexual relationship.

Some sex games could be inappropriate. If the couple decides that it is time to bring a sex game into their bedroom, adult sex games, require a cautious approach. If the couple is not ready for a game night, they may not be ready for a sex game in their bedroom. Games are always better when they begin by allowing couples to build up a comfortable and sensual tension to get them into the mind frame for playing.

Why Sex Games Are Important for Your Sexual Life?

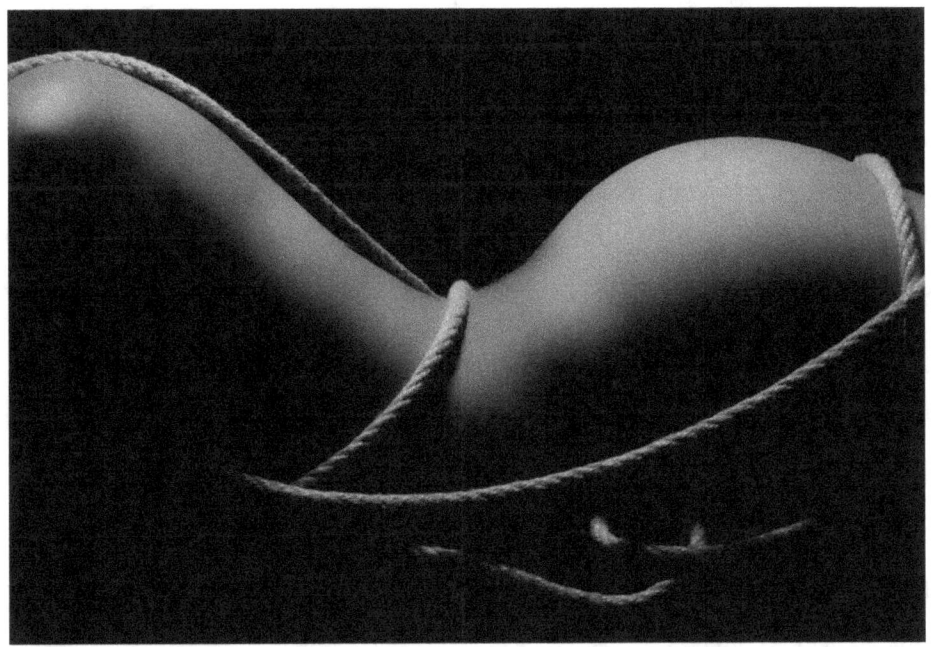

You can get many benefits when you introduce sex games to you and your partner, which are the following:

Rediscovery

This is the first reason sex games are so beneficial for your sex life. Often when we drift from our partners sexually or have decreased interest in them sexually, it's because we feel a distance from them in general. In other words, it's not necessarily a sex problem; it's a relationship problem.

You may be well aware that sex is just one of the symptoms of an underlying cause. Regardless, sex games will help you tackle both the symptom and the underlying cause.

Sex games force you to laugh, work, and think together towards a common goal. It's this simple act of spending time engaging with someone in this way, and having fun that many people have forgotten. Imagine you are reading about one of the sex games from later in this book, and you are gasping from laughter while trying to figure out how to best adapt it to your situation. When's the last time you did that with your partner? That's the rediscovery of them as the fun-loving person you fell in love with, not the person who works too much and sometimes makes a mess in the bathroom sink. Having fun together leads to rediscovery, and sex games are nothing if not fun.

Novelty

Of course, the novelty and allure of something new is also a major part of sex games. This is the feeling of first-time discovery rather than rediscovery.

Your sex life might be boring simply because it's boring. It might be too routine. You might want to try out kinks and fetishes that you saw in pornography. You might not even know what you like, so you want to try out as much as possible.

The pleasure of novelty in sex is well-documented both scientifically and anecdotally. For example, are you more likely to be turned on when your partner has new sexy underwear, or when they whip out sexy underwear that you've seen dozens of times? That same lust for novelty is transferred over to the sex itself.

Sex games allow and push you to experience things you would never have thought of. If imagination isn't your strong suit, just leave that to me. I'll take care of that part and give you more than you can handle! You never know when you might see something that catches your eye and uncovers a trigger for your best orgasms. If you have the same type of sex with the same routines and the same lack of creativity over and over, it's easy to understand why your sex life is suffering. Try out some games and make it spicy and exciting again.

Tension

What is tension in this context? Tension is the feeling of anticipation for something that motivates you toward it. Sexual tension is created when you have the desire, but can't necessarily take care of it at that moment.

Sexual tension is an important part of fulfilling sex life. Without it, you likely have no desire.

Sex games create sexual tension because that's how I've designed them! They are designed to open your mind and do something where sex might not even be the end goal. But, without your realization, you are more turned on and aroused by the game, until the sexual tension boils over and you just want to rip your partner's clothes off. Take the most obvious example of a sensual massage. Your partner orders you to strip naked for a full body massage and soaks your body in oil. They also strip naked. The point here isn't necessarily to have sex, but once the hands start gliding everywhere, it's probably where it will lead.

Effort

Perhaps above all else, sex games represent intentional time and effort spent in the pursuit of better sex life. This is the most important part of fulfilling sex life — the notion that you must work at it, and it's not a given for compatible people. Many people assume that if their sex life with their partner is not naturally orgasmic, then it's a sign of the wrong partner.

How to Introduce Sex Games in Your Bedroom

You desire to venture the feeling of being excited about playing sexual games to flavor up your relationship. But there is only one problem. How do you convince your partner to participate in the idea of playing a couple of games with your partner? Will they agree to play this kind of game or be offended by the fact that you think your sex life is inadequate and boring? This is mostly true in long-term relationships; the idea of talking or modifying your sexual routine can also be inconvenient. But engaging in adult games can be a great way to bring new activities into your love life without feeling embarrassed.

Everyone wants fun and great sex life full of romantic intimacy, erotic adventures, new emotions, and creative foreplay, and that makes them stronger. But most couples are not comfortable about telling the real deal of their sexual wants and needs. Most of the time, we just need a signal that it's okay to be alive, playful, and bad, to give us the approval to release controls over our sexual desire. The key is to start neutral by playing regular games first to build trust and confidence. Then increasingly switch to other levels of play, including more intimate desires.

This is a list of different varieties of adult-themed games with different levels of intensity. Try some games for each level or category before trying the next level. Adjust the speed you are going and be ready to level up if any of you stray too far from your comfort zone, sexually. Common games like cards, checkers, pool, and bowling let you play and have some good times together innocently. Try to make your partner comfortable with playing, and then crave the bet with a nice reward for the one who wins. Come up with a simple striptease if you seed that the mood is on and right.

Sexy games are made your emotional bond stronger by slowing it down and experiencing a connection with each other that is intimate. This can be real books or board games with questions and romantic activities. Also, a sensual massage or a shower gel for two can make feelings that are intense and erotic between you. These loving exercises will increase your confidence level so that you both feel secure with each other. Adult-themed erotic sex games can be fun, based on curiosity, or to wake up your mind. Obtaining more knowledge about sex and observing how your loved one deal with certain erotic issues can make you a more sensitive, sensible partner.

Camera games offer methods to blend different types of sensual pleasure. These playful foreplay acts let you playfully hold and postpone sex while you induce arousal and excite yourself in different ways. This will make one motivated to try new sexual techniques and positions which you may not be able to do if you are not part of the instructions of the game. Be more watchful of what you like and build your confidence in creative lovemaking expertise.

Roleplaying games are intermediate sexual games in which you explore secret desires and fantasies. You can unleash your inhibitions and let go of shyness by pretending and getting into different characters doing acts of erotic and sensual scenes. Maybe you can start by mimicking scenes from books and movies. Try them out using only your imagination before buying accessories and costumes.

Playing and having fun with each other is great for your relationship all the time. When sex games and having fun bring you great feeling pleasure and extraordinary sex, both of you are on the correct path. Building and gaining confidence can be started slowly, and you will see that your partner will greedily explore games and fantasies with you.

How to Introduce Sex Games in Your Bedroom?

Unspoken discontent, unresolved problems, or accumulated aggression—all this must not be in your family life, because they are followed by quarrels, resentment, and a cold and insipid bed. Sexual games are a way to get rid of daily stress, get pleasure, support sensuality and sexuality, and at the same time not offend each other, but rather ignite. Role-playing games in bed make it possible to transform into a character and act as you would never dare in everyday life. This transformation makes it possible not to be shy, not to select words and actions, because you both understand that this is only a game.

Role-playing in bed can solve some family problems. How does it work? Roles for the game can be very different, the plot is much more important. For example, in each couple, one partner always dominates. In the role-playing game, you have the opportunity to switch places: if the husband takes decisions in everyday life, then become a strict teacher and punish him for his bad behavior. Also, a common problem in relationships, when we release the anger and discontent accumulated over the day on a partner, although a loved one is not to blame for your failures at work or other individual areas of life. So that problems outside the home do not be reflected in the relationship, transfer them to the game. If a man comes home after a heated debate with his boss, let him be the boss that night and to write you a few reprimands.

Preparing for a role-playing game: script, rules, and inventory

First of all, think about the difficulties and innuendos in your life with your partner. If you have never played erotic games before, this approach will help you pick up the first roles and relieve tension in the plane of relations where it has accumulated. Incorrect roles or scripts can ruin everything. Imagine a man is constantly depressed due to the fact that his girlfriend has been you swear at him with the reason and without, and here he is offered to play mistress and her page-boy—the same situation that usually. Even if a man agrees, this game is unlikely to bring him pleasure, which, as in any sexual intercourse, should be mutual.

Try to carefully lead your partner to what worries him, to identify painful points, catch random phrases, but you should not talk about it openly, because you risk turning everything into a small home scandal, rather than a fun game. Select the roles that would enable you or your partner to "recoup." It will not be superfluous to learn about his fantasies, but absolutely everyone has them.

So that the game does not come to a standstill or go in the wrong direction (for example, you should have been mistress, and then the man took the initiative again), write a simple, uncomplicated scenario. It is not necessary to think through all the dialogues to the smallest detail, but the general direction should be determined.

Sexy outfits play an important role in erotic games.

Another option to decide on the roles is to delve into yourself: think about what you would like to try, what erotic fantasies visit you, what kind of dress or atmosphere you like most.

The following stage is—outfits. Dressing up is a lot of fun. And understanding what kind of clothes can arouse your sexual desire can make this activity even more fun and enjoyable. Even the most ordinary objects can be filled with sexual vibration. Everything is simple here - either rummage through your own closet in search of suitable clothes (for example, you will definitely find something for the role of a teacher or boss) or look into a sex shop (not every house has a nurse's robe or a pilot's uniform). When you have figured out the costumes, think about what equipment may be needed so as not to run around the apartment in the middle of the game in search of a pointer, stethoscope, or pipi aster—everything should be at hand

Mandatory Role-Playing Rules

The game begins a few hours before the action. Send a thematic message to your partner (for example, "Doctor, I have a headache, can I make an appointment with you tonight?")-At this moment you are already playing, so exclude the everyday messages "Buy bread. "Similarly, you can throw a secret note to your partner, but you need to make sure that he will find it. It will be a shame if you put it in your trouser pocket, and he put on jeans.

- **Do not start if you are not sure that you will reach the end.** The worst thing is to tease each other with messages during the day and change your mind at the last moment. Such turns will not benefit your relationship.
- **Do not change clothes and do not get ready in front of each other.** You should meet for the first time already in full uniform and outfits, otherwise, the "magic" will not work.
- **Play to the end.** None of the partners in the middle of the game can take off the suit and get out of the role. Firstly, sex runs the risk of passing as usual, and not playing the psychological role for which, everything was started. Secondly, you can offend the efforts of a partner, which will only aggravate problems in the relationship.
- **Improvise.** If you initially did not have a ready-made script, or it was not implemented, and the game slows down, do not freak out. It's better to think in advance where the plot might go, and what to do in such cases. In any case, even if you found the problem of interpersonal communications during the game, do not concentrate on it, urgently turn your attention to any aspects that pleasantly excite you in this situation, move the focus to the exciting details, to immerse yourself in the game deeper and not lose your sexual mood. You can reflect and gently argue all points for improvement afterward, in a more suitable atmosphere.
- **Do not try to be a great actor.** To read the monologues from Hamlet in front of the partner is completely unnecessary. Focus on the main goal of the game—quality sex. If you are playing not as George Clooney, believe me, the partner is unlikely to notice this and certainly will not criticize you.
- **Do not go over the role of others.** If the partner dominates in the scenario, do not drag the blanket over yourself. Similarly, if you

dominate, —do not let the partner go over you, you will have to be tougher, but do not go too far—for inexperienced players, the line is rather thin. It's best to clarify the rules in advance.
- **Do not undress ahead of time.** If you threw off clothes from each other at the very beginning, the game already failed, because the very interesting stage of flirting was lost.
- It may sound corny, but some erotic games, especially with the use of BDSM toys, **require to have "stop" words.** The word should be simple, but atypical for the script. If you play, for example, in a clinic, then you should not choose a "dropper" with a stop word, it's better to choose something out of the ordinary, for example, a "bullfighter"—it's unlikely that you were going to deliberate the bullfight in the script.
- **It is preferable that you will be home alone at this time**; the phones should be shut down.
- **You should be as tactful as possible**, sometimes even an innocent joke can bring down the whole mood, and then the partner in the future will completely refuse such entertainments.
- **Don't think about anything extraneous,** if at the height of the game a kitty instead of "murmur" suddenly says that tomorrow she needs to call on her mother, then this greatly disturbs the mood.

Role-Playing Sex Games

In-Flight Rendezvous

What Do You Need?

Make sure to set up the scenario in advance. Put on your sexy and skimpy flight attendant uniform, with high heels, lingerie, and stockings. Put some props like what you usually see in an airplane like cups, napkins, snacks, drink tray, and amenities given to passengers like eye cover, blanket, and neck pillow. Of course, have your handcuffs ready too.

How to Play?

Tell your partner you planned an exciting game where he would act as a flight passenger, and you are the flight attendant who's going to give him lessons about the right conduct in an airplane.

As a flight attendant, tend to the passenger and ask him if he wants some drink or food, then make him do things that will annoy you like spilling drinks, asking too much, and being demanding. Once you get too upset, have your partner kiss and touch you inappropriately. When you are fed up, say to him that you will be needing to restraint him, get your handcuffs out, and put them on his hands placed behind his back. It's your turn now to take control of the game by doing what you like by tease or by showing your breast, touching his penis until it becomes hard. Make demands to him, and he must follow and make sure all are met, and you are satisfied. You can also punish him by removing his clothes waist down and arouse him using your lips, mouth, and hands. Once you see that he's about to cum, stop to tease him more.

Act as Director and A Porn Star

What Do You Need?

Make a scenario of a photoshoot complete with a sofa with fur, or a bed with silk sheets, or a rug in front of a fireplace. Set aside many sex toys and other props you can use. Let your partner wear her bikini or lingerie and wear a robe over it.

Put the film on your camera and additionally set up your camcorder or handheld camcorder. Dress up like it seems that this is true. If you really like your photographs to look valid, purchase a couple of pornography magazines and study the photographs.

How to Play?

This game is a great one for both of you as one gets to play an aspiring porn star or Playboy magazine model, and one gets to play as a director. Now, let's get the camera rolling! Instruct your partner that she must follow all your instructions since she's' new at this career.

Make your partner pose provocatively, sexy, and sensual. Tell her to remove some of her clothes, play with herself, expose her bum, lean over suggestively, and expose her lady parts by pulling her lingerie a little bit to the side. To make it wilder, have her wear handcuffs while you insert some sex toys in her vagina or anus (if she agrees). Get a shot for every pose she makes and compiles them to be watched by both of you afterward.

Serviced By A Housemaid

What Do You Need?

For the costume you will be wearing, you may opt to wear a loose housedress but with sexy lingerie underneath or wear a skimpy French maid uniform with gloves, white cap, apron, and feather duster.

How to Play?

Tell you, partner, to get home early, and once he's home, encourage him to relax on a chair. This time make sure to tend to him like a maid does, giving him something to drink and eat. After this, you'll tell him that you have something that will energize him. Go into your room in a reserved and shy away and start cleaning up, but looking at him provocatively once in a while. From here, you can do a smalls striptease revealing your lingerie underneath, or if you're wearing the maid costume, you can remove it piece by piece and still treat him for a striptease show of his own.

Sit beside your guy and ask him if there is anything that is needing special attention—say you are at his service and will do anything he will ask for. Maybe he needs assistance in removing his clothes so you can put them in the laundry, or would he like you to turn on the television for him? Remove his clothing and leave the room. When you come back, tell him that it should be you pleasing him and give him oral sex.

A Maiden and A Pirate

What Do You Need?

You will need a pirate costume for this one, whether by making one on your own or by purchasing one. Don't forget the smallest of details like the bandana wrapped on your head, darkened eyes with a patch, unbuttoned white polo, tights, and pirate boots. If you want to go all-in, you can also use props like a pet parrot or hook for a hand

How to Play?

Inform your partner that you prepared a swashbuckling game for the two of you. You'll be playing as the pirate, and she will be a captive maiden. Make her dress up like one with a low-cut dress full skirt with no undergarments and several pearl pieces of jewelry. Start the game by saying, "Ahoy, mates! Get your hands off the Captain's maiden!" Pretend to rescue her from other pirates, and you want her all to yourself. Pull her to your lap, stroke her hair, and lay a kiss on her breast. Put your hands under the skirt and finger here and reach for the G-spot.

Another scenario can be: You're one horny pirate, and she's a captive. Tie both of her hands and do anything to here like sucking her breast, ripping her clothes off, and licking parts of her body. For added pleasure, kiss her roughly while pulling her hair back.

Personal Sex Slave

What Do You Need?

Put on your best mistress outfit- a leather or latex bikini or lingerie, choker, decorative belt, and armbands. For your partner, make him dress up with old ragged clothes, or he can be totally naked. Don't forget other props like a choker for him, handcuffs, and a blindfold.

How to Play?

If he likes being dominated, tell your partner you have something prepared for him. You'll both play the role of a mistress and a slave. As a slave, he must do whatever you will order him to do. Give orders like letting him feed you by hand, massaging your scalp or feet, and let it progress to giving you pleasure. Order him to fondle your breast, suck on your nipples, adore your bum and tell him not to stop until you say so.

Afterward, switch roles and make him handcuff you. As his slave, he can order you anything he pleases like giving him oral sex or letting him enter you anally or just anything under the sun.

Classic Erotic Games

If the idea of role-playing games does not inspire you, you can resort to simple erotic games for two. Playing in bed with a partner is a great way to spend time and release accumulated stress.

Naked Blind

Do not worry, this is just a game using improvised things, the name of which the partner may not even guess. You won't believe how many simple household items can be adapted for erotic games—from a dust brush (clean, of course) to a kitchen spatula! Make sure yourself. Sit down or put your beloved on the bed with your back on top, and take such a position so that he does not see either you or what is in your hands. It is better to blindfold him to create a hotter and more interesting atmosphere (so the guy will be able to express his wishes more frankly to you).

Take anything that catches your eye (lipstick, a cool tube of cream, a comb, ice cubes from the refrigerator), and begin to caress your man, asking "yes or no?" If the partner likes it, continue in the same vein, if not—time to change the means at hand. Do it slowly, gently, slightly teasing both, him and yourself.

You will be surprised how many ways can be invented to give pleasure to a partner using the pieces that we use in everyday life. A banal massage comb or a silicone kitchen spatula is ideal for light flip flops on the buttocks, and ice cubes can be completely crazy if you touch the nipples. Unleash your imagination, and then swap places. Are we in for fair play?

Sex-Timer

It's time to remember what foreplay is! If you and your partner usually do not focus on the foreplay and prefer to go directly to the main part, then both of you will be pleasantly surprised by the effect if you change priorities. This will help the game with a timer. You can set the time on the phone or buy a special timer in a sex shop, which can far ahead be used for various speed love games.

The task of that particular game is that you both have to caress each other, without going beyond the "below the belt." You should enjoy every touch, every kiss, every stroking and whispering in your ear, keeping your hands on the most interesting places and not moving on to penetration until the alarm rings. This game will evoke memories of how great it is to just kiss, teasing, and maximally inflame each other's desires.

Erotic Forfeits

A game following the example of classic forfeits for completing tasks, but in our case, it will be erotic desires. It is better to buy a ready-made set of forfeits, where everything is thought out for you, but you can try to make them yourself, agreed with a partner.

What Tasks to Add

To be fair, the number of cards should be equal, and it is advisable to take the paper of different colors (the classic version is pink and blue) so that during the game you understand where women's desires are and where men's desires are.

Formulate your erotic "want" together. For example, you write "do me a buttock massage" or "I am your captive" (this means that he will be able to do whatever he wants with you). And he writes "I want you to be a bad girl" (here the role of "do whatever you want" goes to you) or briefly "69" (where everything is clear without clarification). It is important not to peek so that all desires come out unexpectedly for you and him.

Put forfeits into a basket and mix them. Then pull out one piece of paper and take turns doing everything that is written there. This game is cool in that you and your partner can share your innermost fantasies without saying a word.

Card Game

You will need a deck of cards and a stopwatch. Give each one a few cards. Each suit means a kind of caress: Hearts—kisses, diamonds—massage, clubs—penetration, and spades—oral caress. Card value means duration in seconds; jacks, queens, and kings—in minutes. Depending on the set that you got, you will have an individual and unpredictable caress program.

Tickling for Strip

Tickle each other in turn. Everyone who started laughing or started to dodge takes off one thing until someone stays completely naked. However, you are likely to switch to sex before the end of the game.

How It Works

Paradoxically, but tickling causes strong arousal, similar to sexual. And your undressing in the process of sexual games for couples makes your arousal quite clearly bright.

Mirror

One partner repeats the actions of the other with maximum similarity. The game is simple but incredibly exciting.

Mind Reading

How to Play?

Undress and sit opposite to each other, look into each other's eyes, trying to read thoughts, and guess what your partner would like you to do with him. After a few minutes, share your observations with your partner, and let him say whether you guessed right or not.

Maybe you will be pleasantly surprised by the wishes of your partner and look at him from a new side. In any case, such a sexual conversation is exclusively erotic and exciting. After it, you can make each other's wishes a reality.

Creative Sex Games

Dress for Sex

While your partner is getting dressed to go somewhere without you, ask him to wear something specific just for you, and promise to do the same thing. She could wear a particularly sexy bra under a very banal T-shirt to visit her parents, while he could put on his silk underpants to go to his parents. Most men would immediately accept this proposal for the simple fact that they will never, and never ever have, another opportunity to wear this kind of clothing, which also puts a lot of leverage on the novelty factor. This game works, despite its simplicity, because during all the time you are separated you will stay focused on having a "spicy" secret to keep.

Tell A Story

Make up an erotic story based on you and your lover—go into as much detail as possible—then write it down and put it in some unexpected place so that they can find it the following day. If you are not good at writing, record it and send it to him on the phone—preferably at a completely inappropriate time.

Become A Shooting Artist

It is definitely worth registering while having sex (if you are silent types, give it some moaning and swearing for the occasion). Feel it as you drive together somewhere where you absolutely have to keep a tone or share headphones on public transport.

Lighting

Turn off the lights and then take turns to light a part of your body with a torch. Each part must be touched, caressed, or licked for two minutes, then the torch passes to the other person. A rule: You cannot illuminate the same part more than once.

Dress Up

PVC nurse clothes, catsuits, Superman equipment, French maid skirts. Disguises like this are very cheap if you search online. Sure, they are tacky and itchy to wear, but anything that turns you into another character is good. It works especially for couples who now feel so close as to think they are having sex between siblings: the role-play pushes you out of the comfort zone towards something more fun and genuine.

The Sexual Therapist
One of you goes to a private place to take the phone call from a 'patient' you are trying to help. The patient, or your lover, pretends to ask for advice on how to satisfy your partner. The therapist at this point begins to unravel a series of dirty details on how to satisfy him, naturally describing your very idea of paradise!

Without Using Your Hands!
Tie your partner's hands together and ask him to seduce you. They will have no choice but to use their lips, teeth, and tongue—or to use ingeniously other parts of their body that they would never have dreamed of associating with sexual intercourse. And if you want to make things really interesting, tie both hands behind your back.

The Guinea Pig Game
Take all the erotic toys you own (order again if you only have a dusty vibrator) and arrange them neatly on a table in the bedroom. Call your lover while out shopping and tell him that you urgently need them as 'guinea pigs' for a project you're working on. When they get home, test each toy on them: they will have to rate it based on the level of pleasure received.

Fantastic Sex Games

Strip Poker

The most fantastic of the erotic games that can be played in the bedroom is strip poker. Often, in fact, one goes in search of very complicated entertainment to stimulate desire, when perhaps the most effective one has been known for decades and can be practiced at any time.

For those few who did not know it, strip poker is a very simple variation of poker in which garments are used instead of chips. So, when you "open" your hand or relaunch your bets, you will have to say you are willing to put your shirt, your bra, or your underwear on the plate. And to give them the item in case you lose it.

Therefore, a few materials are enough to play with it. Obviously, you need poker cards and knowledge of the rules of the game but above all an identical number of clothes. If the woman of the couple wears more clothes than the man, it is probable, he must put on something else to balance the bill.

In addition, the game is especially fun if you manage to create the right atmosphere. We suggest a suitable and intimate environment, such as that of the bedroom. The lights must be soft enough so that you can see the fruit of your winnings but without making everything too loud.

Finally, when you lose a hand and are forced to take something off you, it would be good to improvise a small striptease. Of course, it will be tastier to see the strip of her socks than his socks, but taking it with a certain irony, even the latter eventuality can be fun.

Erotic Dice

If you don't like card games, you can get rid of the playful aspect and go directly to penances. In specialized and online stores you will find, for example, dice that have been specially made to give you some interesting ideas. There are various types and they cost a few euros, but if you want you can also create them yourself. Just use, for example, traditional dice and a conversion table (1 corresponds to a penance, 2 to another, and so on).

What can be found, however, in the various faces of these dice? For example, in one there can be actions and in the other the parts of the body. To be more concrete, in the first verbs such as "kiss," "suck," "pinch," "touch," "blow" or "lick" and in the second areas such as "chest," "lips," "ears," "neck," " sit," "navel" (or even worse, if you want).

Other dices, however, provide suggestions on sexual positions, like Kamasutra. They are often dicing with 8, 10, or 12 faces with real explanatory drawings on the various sides. Rolling the dice, therefore, can force you to try things that have never been experienced before.

Monogamy

This is the first real erotic box game ever made. It is called Monogamy; it is produced by the British Creative Conceptions and is easily found in online stores. The game offers a game board with a circular path to be used by your pawn, and as you end up on the various squares you run into different cards. These cards —100 for him and 100 for her— each present 3 questions, with 3 different game levels. In addition, there are also 50 fantasy cards.

The questions, in particular, allow us to investigate the couple's alchemy, and prove to be spot on both for the partners who have been together for a long time, and for the novices. In part, these are questions that investigate the other's mind, in part, they suggest moving to action instead.

Erotic Twister

Monogamy is a game that must be purchased, and that must somehow wait for you to get home. If, however, it comes to your mind at the last moment, when it is already evening, to try an erotic game, you can orient yourself on a different solution. Use a classic box game, changing the rules.

This can be done with all games, perhaps with specific penances. Let's say that in Monopoly you don't have the money to pay when you pass over Victory Park: maybe your partner can give you a discount in exchange for some caresses.

However, there is also a game that already in its basic version is very suitable for an erotic evening: Twister. Remember it? It is that game in which a carpet with colored circles is placed on the ground, and then, by turning a small arrow on a dial, you understand where you need to put your hand or foot.

Obviously, when we play in many we end up meeting in improbable and improper poses. But in two poses they can also become subtly erotic. If the normal Twister is not enough for you, you can change the rules. Maybe placing a colored circle also on some sensitive areas of the body ("right hand on green buttock").

Tickling

In some areas of the world, in fact, this ancient practice has come back into fashion with the aim of preparing the couple for sexual intercourse. Tickling, in fact, allows you to create the right intimacy between partners and to touch in parts of the body that are not immediately sexual, but nonetheless erogenous.

You don't even have to use your fingers, but you can use other tools. For example, a feather passed on the neck (maybe behind) or on the back can have a particularly exciting effect. Some films then taught us the usefulness of using ice cubes, silk ribbons, or even hair to caress our partner.

In this case, the important thing is to explore the other's body and find out which are the most receptive and sensitive points, in order to stimulate them adequately. Furthermore, the ideal would be to postpone the passage "to the facts" as much as possible, in order to enjoy this long but vibrant wait.

Lust

We told you about Monogamy, the perfect box game for couples. Well, that's not the only one you can use if you want to liven up an evening. Another available on the market is called Lust, and it is no coincidence that it is presented as a "Passion Play," a game of passion.

The game involves two players, who, through cards or specific moves, arrive at the end of a game by getting the suggestion of some sexual positions to explore.

There are many combinations, more than 30,000, so that every time you can venture into an ever new experience.

Erotic Heart

Erotic Heart is also based on more or less the same principles, another game for couples that are actually marketed under various different names depending on the importer. However, its name is due to the fact that it is presented, right from the box, in a heart-shaped container.

Inside there are several rolled up notes, which the partners can fish one at a time. In each one is indicated a penance, but a very sweet penance, since it has an erotic nature that will surely be appreciated by the companion or companion.

Soft Bondage

There are also easier games to put into practice, for which there is no need to spend money or go to some shop. For example, bondage, practiced for a very long time even with very simple objects, such as ribbons or handkerchiefs (or even handcuffs and ropes, when you want to do things big).

Well, the game can be nice, especially if done in an undemanding way. In fact, soft bondage does not involve dangerous bonds, but only a few small games with laces and ribbons, preferably made of silk, in which to pretend and simulate even a little.

Smeared Food

Have you seen 9 1/2 weeks? The scene in which Mickey Rourke passes an ice cube over Kim Besieger's body is famous in that film. It is a very erotic scene, which at the time many tried to replicate even in the closet of their bedroom.

You don't have to use ice, actually. Indeed, with other elements—and in particular with food—the experience can be even more intriguing. Think for example of whipped cream, or strawberries, which are also aphrodisiac. In short, even here the fantasy is the master.

Erotic Apps

If your imagination doesn't really help to invent new sex games, you can resort to some erotic apps to install on your smartphone. For example, there is Planet Porn, a wide selection of videos and free images to whet your imagination, while for couple's sex games you can choose between Ultimate Sex Games for Couples for iPhone and The Foreplay Game for Android. If you want to try tantric sex instead, there is a Tantric Sex Deck. The important thing is that the apps are helpful for experimenting. The phone must not become an annoying third party! Unless you decide to use it for sexting: if a couple is forced to stay away, they can still carve out a spicy moment. In fact, at a distance, you can exchange sexy images, perhaps through an app that does not leave a mark like Snapchat, and messages with high erotic content. The only precaution is to always be attentive to privacy and to do sexting only with a person you trust, in order to avoid unpleasant inconveniences such as the diffusion of photos and screenshots of the chats.

Kissing Games

Sexy Mood Match Game

What Do You Need?

With your partner, come up and list different sets of foreplay acts for every 13 values of the card from King to Ace of a standard deck of cards.

Next is to Shuffle and deal out all the cards facing down so that you and your partner will have equal halves of the deck. Make sure no one peeks.

How to Play?

This game is a hot and sexy version of the Snap Card Game. This is a quick sex game where sensual foreplay, hot make-out session, and stripping can happen if you both have matching cards. Each type of card is representing an erotic foreplay act that both of you desire. Take turns in giving foreplay to each other to get both of you horny for the main event. Between the two of you, the one who gets to win more cards will receive an extra sexual reward or favor—which will depend on what you wish to experience.

Both players will turn over their first card from the stack at the same time and put them facing up next to each other. Look if these two cards match. If it does not match, continue to flip over cards until cards match. At this point, both of you must shout the sexy mood is matching the cards. The on one shout first will win that foreplay. Instead of snap, shout the following words:

- If two cards are both red, shout "Lick."

- If two cards are both black, shout "Suck."

- If two cards are both red & black, shout "Fuck."

But in those instances where you shout the words at the same time, you must both perform the act to each other.

If you call out the cards wrong, you must face a punishment, which is the following.

You must strip off a piece of your clothes and surrender your cards to your partner if you called out the wrong type of matching cards. But no one among you will receive a sexual act or foreplay. If one of you is completely naked, you need to surrender your deck of cards.

If you did shout a match, but it does not exist, you must do the corresponding foreplay act as indicated by the top card of your partner. In this instance, you can keep your cards.

Shuffle and turn over cards facing down when one of you runs out of cards then continue the game. You can play this for a limited time of 10 to 20 minutes per set or per round or until will win most cards. The person with the most collected cards at the end of the game will win and will receive their special sexual favor or reward to be performed by the loser.

Q-P   Hug and passionately kiss each other.

P-Q   Massage any part of your body.

Q-N   Tenderly stroke, caress and kiss an exposed erogenous zone.

N-Q   Kneeling, kiss, and lick your belly, hips, and thighs.

Q-B   Enjoy as you caress and fondle your partner's body.

B-Q   Expose and allow you to lick and suck their nipples.

Q-R   Sensual manual genital stimulation.

R-Q   Stimulate you with a sex toy (visual stimulation counts)

Q-Q   Ladies' choice of any foreplay activity for both of you.

Q-K   Orally pleasure you.

K-Q   Ass play—sensual spanking, massage, butt plug, etc.

You and your partner can play as many rounds as you can, and I suggest you come up with a different set of foreplay acts per game.

Maybe you can also do another element of stripping clothes by making Jokers part of the deck cards. If both of you get matching jokers, the word to shout is "Strip." The one who says it last will need to remove his clothing using one hand.

Queens Gone Wild

What Do You Need?

For a two-player game, prepare a regular chess board complete with its pieces. With your partner, make a list of different activities involving foreplay when a piece takes a queen or vice versa. Do write down erotic rewards for each piece that has the chance to take the King to finish the game.

How to Play?

This erotic variation of chess is a foreplay game for your mind and body. In this couple's game, you'll focus on your queen. Play your queen right and your partner will do some stripping off clothes and pleasure you. Just like most women, in this game, your queen gets to play more than once. She won't stop until you both reach satisfaction.

The main goal of the game is to let the King mate with the queen. You'll both have great rewards when you play with your queen a lot more because this is where foreplay happens. Make sure to take the queen to have more erotic activities.

Foreplay Activities Performed by Your Partner

Sex Play Rewards

P-K   Genital massage to orgasm using lube.

B-K   Intercourse missionary style.

N-K   Intercourse doggie style.

R-K   Oral sex to orgasm while using a vibrator.

Q-K   Intercourse in any woman on top position.

K-K   Anal intercourse (winner's choice).

Make use of the classic rules of chess with a few modifications related to how the King and queen are played with. When you take a piece with your queen, your lover pleasures you according to the type of piece taken. And, when you get the queen.

- Strip of any garment you have on.
- The queen will be placed anywhere on the half of your board by your partner.
- Your lover pleasures you depending on the way the queen was taken.

Essentially any activity involving your queen means your lover pleasures you in some way. The queen takes the queen's situation is special. In this case, either choose one activity for both of you or take turns pleasuring each other.

You must move out of check unless you're in checkmate or stalemate, in which case you must still make a move with the King before he's taken. Once the King has been taken, the one winner will be receiving a special sexual reward based on the last piece of the game.

Play multiple games if you like to have foreplay of different intensities.

Bump and Grind

What Do You Need?

For this game, you will need a Sorry! At the start, both of you must behave complete clothes on, ideally five layers and articles on to make the game longer and the sexual tension long. Afterward, sit together and make a list of sexual acts or foreplay acts for each card value, in this case, 11, and then mutually agree on the ultimate sexual reward of the victorious one.

How to Play?

This erotic and sexy version of the board game Sorry will have you, and you're loved on strip off clothes and act out several foreplays that will make you aroused and excited, to start the game, gather your pieces and put them around the board and home in able to win this and great sex waiting. When playing, every time you "bump "your partner, you bring them back to start, and you must say Sorry, but in this version, a little playful fondling will do the trick. Apart from that, you must let them take off a piece of their clothing whenever you send it back to start.

In playing this version, we will just some variation on the standard rules of the usual sorry game.

- Do the corresponding act of foreplay for your partner when you play a card, and you bumped your partner's piece.
- You must remove a piece of clothing to get ready for more fun to come in the event that you get to bring a piece of their home.

Crisscross Applesauce

What Do You Need?

All you need is a fingernail, feather, or other small, gentle scratching device for creating the shivers. Set up a sensual spot for exploration and keep some paper and a pen nearby for taking notes. Get naked together in whatever way you desire or come to the game undressed.

How to Play?

Remember the children's game Crisscross Applesauce? Then you know the goal of this game: to bring out the shivers on your lover's body. Have your lover lay flat on his stomach. Straddle his bottom, sitting on his rear end or lower back. Whisper this rhyme as you make the movements in parentheses:

Crisscross (draw an X on his back)

Applesauce (rub his back lightly in a circular motion with several fingernails)

Spiders crawling up your back (walk your fingernails up his back)

Spiders here (tickle gently under his left arm),

Spiders there (and under his right)

Spiders even in your hair (lightly tickle his neck, hairline, and head)

Cool breeze (blow softly at his neckline),

Tight squeeze (squeeze his neck or shoulders)

Now you've got the shivers! (Run your fingernails up and down his back or anywhere close by) As you draw the X on his back, gently sweep your clitoris and labia across his buttocks. Brush your breasts across his lower back as you walk your fingers up his back. As you blow softly on his neckline, run a finger down his spine, around his buttocks, and back up the crevice; alternatively, whisper "hot air" on his neckline and press your breasts into his back. For variation, use the Crisscross Applesauce game on your lover as he lies on his back and alters the words and movements to discover where he gets the most goosebumps sunny side up.

Guess the Flavor

What Do You Need?

Candy with different Flavors like Jolly Ranchers or Skittles, Water.

How to Play?

Eat a piece of candy without letting your partner see the color or flavor of it. After eating it, let them kiss you and make them guess what flavor it is. Take turns. Whoever loses will give oral sex to the winner.

Oral Sex Games

The Sixty- Nine Ball Game

What Do You Need?

Balls or a Pool Table.

How to Play?

This is a sexy, dirty version of the game Nine Ball. For this version, a lot of sensual foreplay, stripping off clothes and oral sex will happen based on your skill or luck. So, the goal of the game is to be the first one to sink the #9 ball. In this game, it is fine if you do not sink the ball in orders, aka 1-9, just hit the target ball first. Anytime you are able to make both sinks and shot balls, you have the right to receive special foreplay from your partner. The winner will be the one first to complete 6 games and oral and will win an erotic reward of complete orgasm by oral sex.

Restaurant Server's Words

What Do You Need?

At least an hour, your usual date night outfit, sex toys you prefer.

How to Play?

The game will happen during a date night in a restaurant. You and your partner will be assigned lines or phrases and actions that you think your server will say or do during the meal. An example would be what a waiter would say when he's greeting you, bringing your drinks. While taking what meals you will order and when gives the bill. Actions and phrases will be given before you go to dinner, and all consequences from those actions will be fulfilled after the dinner, and you're home.

- "My name is _____, and I'll be serving you tonight = Blowjob for him.
- "For our special, I recommend the _____ dish = Finger with Licking.
- "Would you love some desserts to finish off your meal? = Combination of Oral sex and toy.

Lucky Card

What Do You Need?

At least 30 minutes of your time, a deck of cards, sex toys.

How to Play?

Each card deck number (1, 2, 3, 4..., Q, K, A etc.) is assigned a specific act connected to you and your partner.

Actions for each Deck, you may modify it too.

Ace — the man, will kiss the man on the lips for 20 seconds

2 — the woman will kiss the man on the lips for 20 seconds

3 — man will kiss and suck a part of the man's body

4 — the woman will kiss and suck a part of the man's body

5 — man will finger the girl

6 — the woman will give handjob

7 — man will lick the woman

8 — the woman will give a blowjob

9 — man's genitals are massaged with a sex toy

10 — woman's genitals are massaged with a sex toy

Jackman is given oral pleasure

Queen — the woman, is given oral pleasure

King — 2 minutes of intercourse (everybody wins)

The Anatomy Test

What Do You Need?

In a room, set up an intimate area for exploring such as a soft, furry rug or a bed with fresh sheets, you and your partner must undress and stay beside each other all naked, or you can also slowly undress each other, it's up to you. Review the different erogenous spots of the body and come up with funny names or codes that can help you remember them. Don't forget your necktie or handcuff, blindfold, and edible body paint.

How to Play?

Now that you are done reviewing the different hotspots of the body, it is time for the anatomy test! Put the blindfold on your partner and tell them to indicate the various erogenous zones of your body using one of their own body parts, particularly one choice among tongue, lips, fingers, or hands. Once done, switch places, if using edible paint; put a mark on those hot spots with a ranking of how sensitive that zone is (1 for inner thigh, 2 for earlobe, 3 for nipples, etc.) Wear the blindfold and tell the numbers out where you want him to fondle using his finger, hand, lips, or tongue.

Bring Out His Pleasure

What Do You Need?

Set up an intimate, erotic scene like a bed with fresh sheets or a rug with pillows in front of a fireplace or candles surrounding it. Make the light a little dim, pop some bottle of wine, prepare toys and lube if you like

How to Play?

Call your partner and tell them you have prepared something specially made for him that he will surely love. What you want to achieve in this game is to delay his orgasm and prolong his sensual reactions or erotic sensations as much as you can. To heat things up, fondle his penis, lick the head, give him a blowjob or kiss and lick him all over. One explosive way to let him feel good is the ancient Chinese method called 3-finger draw. While giving him a blowjob, find the perineum, the area between the anus and testicles, then make a curve with your fingers and slightly apply pressure to it. This technique will make things hotter and harder for him.

Sex Games with Drinks

It Takes Two to Tango

When we come to the point of talking about alcoholic drinks and sex games, one can't resist the opportunity to think about the different classic hot sex games you can do. To start, one just needs to have an empty bottle; it can be a bottle of your preferred booze. Simply turn the bottle around and act out the one being asked for. When the bottle points to your partner, different types of kisses must be given to you. Also, in the event that you need to add somewhat more flavor to the game, you can utilize whipped cream or chocolate spread which of course will depend on what flavor you preferred and if the end of the bottle points to your partner, he must lick it from your body and indulge in whatever food you chose to heighten up the sexual anticipation.

Sexy Coin Toss or Heads or Butts

The classic game of coin toss is transformed into a hot, sexy, and dirty version that couples will love. At each flip of the coin, both of you must bet opposite, guessing if it will heads or butts. The one who fails to think it correctly must drink one shot and take off one piece of clothing they have on. The games end when one of you is already fully naked, which will then pave the way to more hot and sexy foreplay.

Boozy Body Shots

One of the most simple and classic sexy booze games, all you need to have would be two pieces of dice, pen, and paper, shot glasses, and your favorite booze. Write on the part of the paper the different areas of the body and fold them, and indicate a number for each piece of paper. The player will then throw the dice and get the corresponding numbered paper. Whatever body part is written is where the shot of booze must be taken from.

Straight Face Is the Game

Provide both of you and your partner a piece of paper, each where you will list 6-12 naughty, dirty, and erotic words you can think of without revealing them to one another. Once done, fold each cut piece of paper and toss them into a bowl.

With each turn, you and your partner will take one piece of paper and try to recite it so anyone can hear without showing even a bit of emotion. In the event that you and your partner can keep a straight face, no consequence will be served. Among the two of you, the one who will show a pinch of emotion, a grin, laugh, or cringe must take one shot.

Hot Vodka Twister

Balance is the main concept of the game Twister, and adding the element of getting drunk will make it more exciting and way more fun. Play the game the usual way, but to make it different, put several vodka shots and some glasses with water on the sheet's number. After spinning, drink the shot on the number before you put your leg or hand on it. Lucky for you, if you drink a shot of water. All this drinking, touching, and getting close to each other's body will surely end up in the bedroom afterward.

Steamy Eye Contact Game (Don't Blink or Else)

Here's your chance to look into each other's eyes deeply without getting awkward. While looking into each other's eyes, you must be still and prevent your eyes from blinking. The one who blinks will need to take a shot and strip off one piece of garment. This game will heighten the feeling of sexual anticipation and tension between the two of you. Maybe you can wear provocative clothes, so you'll make it more difficult for them to concentrate looking into your eyes.

Body Treasure Map (X Marks the Spot)

If you are looking for a chance and a reason to kiss your love, now is the best timing for that. In this game, your main goals are to remember where you want to be kissed and licked with their lips and tongue. Give your partner 4 chances in guessing where your preferred X spot is. If they are correct in guessing, then lucky for you because you'll be receiving some kissed and licking on that spot, but if they were not able to guess, they have to take 3 shots of your chosen booze. Keep playing, guessing, and kissing all you want until the both of you are horny and drunk to finish it off in the bedroom.

Striptease Q&A

The first step in this game is for you to think of one word, may it be a thing, person, place, animal, or emotion. Don't reveal the word to your partner yet. Give them three chances in guessing the word and let them ask you questions that you can answer with a yes and no for them to have clues. For each question they ask, they must give an answer, and if it wrong, your partner must take a shot and kiss you somewhere you like. If, in the end, they were not able to give the word, your partner must do lap dance and striptease for you, and of course, you know what comes next.

Blinded Erotic Touch

Blindfolds are known as one of the most erotic things you can use in doing foreplay and seduction. The reason behind this can be that when other senses are blocked, the remaining senses will be more sensitive. All feelings will be intensified, and a simple touch before will feel more intense when blindfolded. Having said this, if you want to make your next drinking session an erotic one, this game is something you must do. The first step is to have one of you blindfolded, then one who isn't will act as the guide and put the index finger on several areas of the body (better if it's the erogenous zones) The one who has blindfold must then guess which body part they are touching. If your partner doesn't give the correct body part, he must take a shot, but if he does, you are the one who needs to take a shot.

Hottest Sex Games

The Bondage Game

What Do You Need?

Get a set of handcuffs or rope, a blindfold, and leg restraints, if it is desired. Line up your favorite lubrication, sex toys, feathers, and other good devices for teasing. Set a sexy scene by building a fire in the fireplace and creating a luxurious and sensual spot for her to lie. Ask her to wear a sexy outfit of her choosing, or buy her a new outfit—every woman loves presents!

How to Play?

When she comes into the room, greet her with a deep, passionate kiss, and tell her how sexy she is. Serve her a drink, and then lead her over to the pleasure zone. Gently restrain her hands and tell her that her job is to lie back and enjoy the ride.

Once she's restrained, it's your turn to tease her as long as you like. Focus on her breasts and work slowly: Fondle and caress her breasts, squeeze and suck on her nipples. Next, move to her buttocks, then her thighs, and finally, her genitals. If you draw out the teasing sufficiently, she may climax as soon as you touch her clitoris!

To make it more erotic, restrain her legs, and add a blindfold. Use your favorite toys as you tease her mercilessly: Use nipple clamps. At the same time, you kiss her inner thighs, insert a vibrating butt plug as you explore her labia with your fingers, or use your tongue around and around her clitoris while you insert a dildo in her vagina. Stimulate each area, but then move away before she even comes close to climaxing.

Why is it Fun?

Send your lover a note or leave a sexy voice mail and tell her you to know she's been working hard and feeling underappreciated. You have a night of pleasure designed to help her unwind—and you'll do all the work! This is something that can bring a new sensation to each other and a way for you to show how good you are in making her reach orgasm!

Dominant or Submissive

What Do You Need?

A pair of handcuffs, a spanking item, and sex toys if you like to include it.

How to Play?

Let your partner know that you want to play robbers and cops together as a form of doing dominance and submission. One of you will play the one who got caught shoplifting, and one will play the cop representing the law, as a cop or the dominant must be in control of the game. You caught here shoplifting, and now you need to arrest your partner. Have them stand in a corner, facing the wall with their arms and hands surrendering. Pat and frisk down their body, taking more time on their waist, bottom, genitals, and breasts. After, handcuff your partner and let them turn around and command him/her to perform oral sex on you or else.

To make it hotter, you can begin with a little game of chasing your partner around the house and catch her then afterward tell them as a cop. You need to do a strip search and slowly remove their clothing while breathing heavily on their neck. Once you are done with your strip search and frisking, command your partner to get down on the ground, legs, and arms on squats, face down. Search your partner in this position and fondle their vagina or penis until they are aroused, either they are wet or hard. Now's the perfect time to perform anal sex with a toy (if consent has been given)

Why is it Fun?

This sexy game of dominance and submission is a fun way to introduce you to this type of kink.

Drop the Dice

What Do You Need?

At least 15 minutes of your time, sex toys and dice

How to Play?

Make two types of list and number them from 1 to 6. For the first list, distinguish six foreplay or sexual moves like kissing, rubbing massaging, biting, sucking and nibbling, and so much more. For the second list, distinguish six erogenous body parts or "areas like ear, navel, lips, areas below and above the waist, etc. Once ready, one of you will roll the first die and the other one to know the corresponding body part from the first list and what sexual activity must be performed. Your loved one "wins" that sexual act or foreplay from you. Once they did what was asked, switch roles. It's your choice of how many rounds you want to perform.

Why is it Fun?

This is one hot way to do foreplay before the main event, and you can get creative as much as you like in making a list with your partner.

Classic Strip Poker

What Do You Need?

Set up a sexy area in your house and a complete deck of playing cards. Try to understand ahead of time the mechanics of the game with your partner. For a classic poker game, every time you fail to win a hand, you have to strip off a piece of the clothes you are wearing. Set up a stash of coins and divide it equally for the two of you.

How to Play?

Start by Dealing out two cards that are facing down and one card facing up. Agree upon a bet (a dollar or fifty cents), then continue by dealing out 3 pieces of cards facing up and the last card facing down. Highest to lowers Winning hands are the following

- The royal flush
- The straight flush
- The flush
- The full house

- Three of a kind
- Two pairs
- One pair.

The one who is victorious of each hand will tell the partner which piece of clothing he needs to remove. Look whether you can go and proceed to do this drawn-out fore playing until one is fully naked, then let the winner make a final decision on what sexual fantasy or act he wants the partner to do. Maybe you can also add erotic elements like using sex toys, or using only hand or lips and tongue to pleasure you.

Another version you can do to make things hotter is by letting the loser perform a type of service like massaging a part of their partner's body, sucking the head of the penis, fingering the pussy, or licking the breast of the winner. Once someone is fully naked, proceed to a sexual fantasy game related to gambling like a gambler having huge amounts of debt to a loan shark, and to repay, he or she must perform a sexual act.

Why is it Fun?

This is a great way to do foreplay and can have lots of variety on what type of punishment and rewards you can give to you and your partner. If you are the type who does not get jealous of seeing your lover do some intimate activities with other people, this can also be a fun and sexy game to play with your friends.

Timed Encounters

What Do You Need?

A phone with a timer or a kitchen timer

How to Play?

Set the timer for a minimum of three minutes or even five minutes. Agree to use those minutes to perform any foreplay you want to do and stop the moment the alarm goes off.

Why is it Fun?

This creates instant arousal for both of you that can finish off with great sex. Not only it excites both of you, but the feeling of being desired within those minutes will also make your libido higher.

Come and Follow the Leader

What Do You Need?

None, just the two of you.

How to Play?

Figure out who is the Follower and who's the Leader. The Leader follows their fingers and tongue everywhere throughout the Follower in the specific way that they desire to be touched or aroused. The Follower at that point needs to make similar moves and recreate them on the Leader. Switch roles the same number of times as you'd like.

Why is it Fun?

This is great in building up sexual tension and anticipation and is a great memory game that can be both fun and erotic for you. To make it hotter, use food like Choco sauce or whipped cream put on your body in patterns he must remember

Rip It Off

What Do You Need?

Lightweight or old tank top, shirt, or underwear you don't mind parting with after the game.

How to Play?

Wear any of the items of clothing given above, and while on the verge of taking off clothes, tell your partner to start ripping off any of the pieces of clothing with either their teeth or hands.

Why is it Fun?

This a great prelude to rough sex, which is a hot way of making love. It fulfills your desire to be wild and barbaric.

Mirroring

What Do You Need?

Props you like, maybe some sex toys.

How to Play?

One partner repeats the actions of the other with maximum similarity. The game is simple but incredibly exciting. How to Play? undress and sit opposite to each other, look into each other's eyes, trying to read thoughts and guess what your partner would like you to do with him. After a few minutes, share your observations with your partner, and let him say whether you guessed right or not. Maybe you will be pleasantly surprised by the wishes of your partner and look at him from a new side. In any case, such a sexual conversation is exclusively erotic and exciting. After it, you can make each other's wishes a reality.

Why is it Fun?

This is one way for you to show your partner how exactly you like to be treated in bed. It's also a great way for you to show them several moves you like to do to them.

The Full Course Meal

What Do You Need?

Different Food and Drinks for each room in your house (you can also make the feel of the room more romantic by using dim lights or candles).

How to Play?

Cook or buy a five-course meal (cocktail or wine, appetizer, then a vegetable dish or salad, a main dish and lastly a dessert) which must be placed in every chosen room in your home. Go to each room and eat what course is inside the room while making an erotic move or foreplay move, and as you progress to other rooms, you must also amp up your move to a higher notch. Maybe start with kissing, stripping each other's clothes, sucking, and some oral foreplay till you reach the main event.

Why is it Fun?

This is a fun activity that will not only make you enjoy food but a great way to build sexual anticipation and tension.

Back to the Beginning

What Do You Need?

Just the two of you.

How to Play

A pretty simple game of trying to bring back or reenact the first you made love. Be detailed from where you had your date, to the place you had sex, and try to reminisce how you first felt.

Why is it Fun?

It's always the honeymoon phase where libido is very high, and it's always good to remind both of you how it's like to be so in love with each other.

The Hiding Spot

What Do You Need?

Cloth to be used as a blindfold, a necktie, or something to tie the hands and your choice of candies.

How to Play?

It's a game of hiding and seeks but on each other's body. Set who's going to be the Seeker and Hider. The Seeker will be blindfolded and his/her hands will be tied and will kneel on the bed while the Hider will get naked and will lay down, placing candies on several areas of their body. Once finished, the Seeker must now search the candies using only his mouth or by kissing

Advanced Sex Games for Adventurous Couples

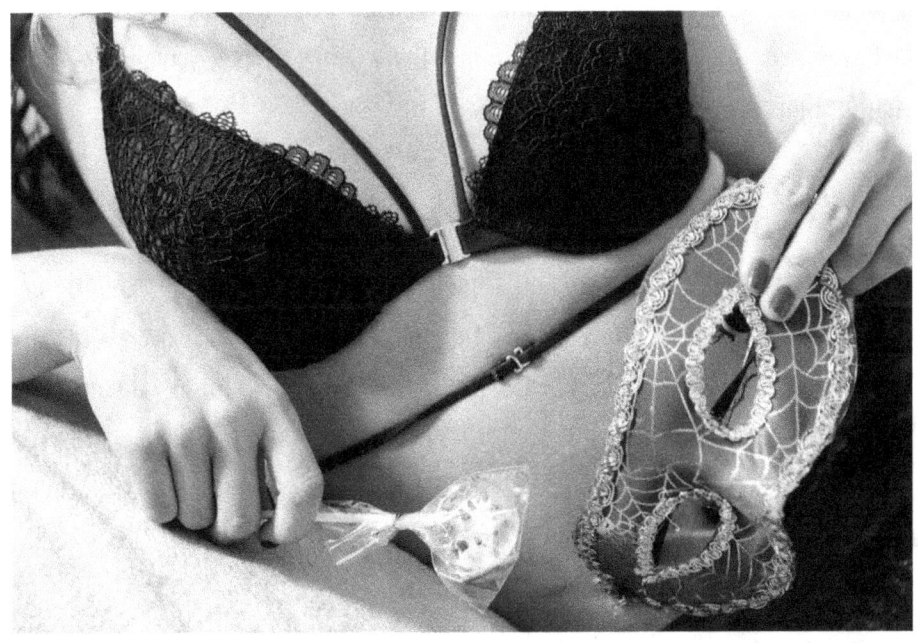

Maybe you and your partner have already been dabbling in sex games and are looking to kick things up another notch, or you simply want to try out some more adventurous games. Well, we've got you covered. There is a research that has found that those who usually engage in new activities like sex games have higher satisfaction levels than couples who don't. Sex games help couples have a more exciting life together.

The games that we will go over will be a mixture of completely free options that will only require your imagination, while others will make you buy something. As always, make sure that you have your partner's consent before trying something new in bed.

Sexy Retail Therapy

For this one, you and your partner will head out for some shopping. You can do this in person or online. You can both pick out something that you would like to see the other one in, or one of you can pick out clothes for the other, whichever way works best for you. Once the clothes arrive, have some fun watching their jaw drop as you get dressed up.

Drive and Dare

We've already talked about how a lot of people find the idea of doing something kinky outdoors or in public is hot. So this game lets you get freaky al fresco. To play this game, both of you need to put on some skimpy clothes. It could be a sexy black dress or some flimsy shorts and a simple t-shirt. Then, go drive for a while. You will take turns suggesting places that you will stop at. When you make a stop, the person who chose the place will be dared by his or her partner to go out and do some naughty things.

Keep the dared low-key to make sure you don't draw a lot of attention to yourself. Then when you start to make the trip back home, start to move your hand up your partner's leg to let them know you want to do something together.

Tear It Up

Have you ever fantasized about having wild, rip off your clothes sex, but didn't want to mess up your own clothes? Then you are going to want to try this game. All you have to do is head out and buy some super-cheap clothes. A secondhand store may be a good option. Wash them up, get dressed, and then let your partner know that they are free to rip them to shreds.

There is a lot of other ways to tear it up. You can both unleash your carnal lust and have a rip-fest, or you incorporate the ripping into a points-based game. It is all up to you. If you love having rough sex, then you are going to love this.

Strip Pong

This takes beer pong to a whole new level. Clear off your dining table and then place six plastic cups in the form of a triangle. Fill up the cups with beer or your favorite alcohol and then take turns trying to toss a ping pong ball into the other person's cups. When a person scores, their partner has to down what is in the cup that the ball landed in and then take off an item of clothing. The person who first gets a ball into all 6 cups will get to ask for something special.

Toy Tease Time

While retail therapy is all about looks, this game gives you the chance to try out the toys you have fantasized about. Again, you can go to a sex store in person or shop online, but purchase some sex toys that you have always wanted to try out. Don't worry if you don't know where to start. To add more fun to this game, make a list of what you have always wanted to try and give it to your partner. They can then buy whichever ones they want that are on that list. Once the items arrive, you can play a little game. You will be blindfolded and on the bed, and your partner will pull out the toys, one at a time, and gently tease you with them. If you are able to guess what it is in three guesses, then they will bring you to orgasm with it.

Position Challenge

If you would like to have a game that will also make sex last longer, this is the best game. The main objective of the game is a simple one, see how many different positions that two of you can do in one sex session before you both reach orgasm. This game will improve the more often you do it, as you can try to top what you did last time.

Seven Minutes in Heaven

Have you ever gotten to enjoy the excitement of trying to squeeze in a quickie before somebody comes in and finds out? This is the game that will help you to recapture that thrill of having only a certain amount of time to do it. Get a timer and set you and your partner a limit of seven minutes. Then find yourself space, like a closet, and see if the two of you can bang out a quickie before your time is up. This can be a thrilling and fun game to bring the two of you closer together.

House Party

The party is all about holding off an orgasm. Nobody can climax until you have banged in every single room in your house. That's all you have to do is try to have sex in each room before you both climax. You can also use this game as a form of foreplay.

The Oral Master

If your foreplay game seems to be lacking, then you could try the oral master game. All you need to do is set a timer for four minutes and see who is able to initiate the most oral sex positions before time is up. Make sure that you keep score, and then you can swap roles to discover who the master of oral sex is. This also gives you the chance to learn a few more oral sex positions, especially if your knowledge has been limited to a kneeling blow job.

Orgasm Race

This game is all about mutual masturbation and is the best game to try to help bring you and your partner closer. Since most people masturbate by themselves, doing that in front of somebody else will heighten your sense of vulnerability and will help to increase your intimacy. This will also allow you to show your partner exactly what it is that you like and how you want it.

In order to have an orgasm race, you will like beside one another and start pleasuring each other. Whichever person climaxes first is the winner and will continue to please their partner until they climax. You can also set the stipulation that the winner gets to request a sexy little treat the next time you do it.

Name the Letter

This is another game that can spice up your oral sex and foreplay. This game is a great way to explore the body of your partner. All you need to do is have them lie down, blindfold them, and then pick your favorite part on them, like their genitals, breasts, or tummy. Then you will gently form a letter onto their skin, making sure you keep the movements teasing and light. If they guess the letter right, they receive one point. Once they get ten correct responses, they get an orgasm, and so you will swap places.

Put It in My Mouth

If you are really looking to up your desire levels, nothing beats the combo of sex and food. In order to play this, get naked, blindfold your partner, and then they will feed you some delicious foods. You can pick out any of your favorite foods, but sweet foods are typically the best when paired with sex, such as strawberries, yogurt, ice cream, cake, or, the classic, chocolate.

Since your partner is blindfolded, the spoon is going to wind up in several places. And there is one simple rule, whatever gets spilled on you, they have to lick it off. You can guide them toward the right spots. This is an amazing game for trust-building, and you are going to love the sensation of having the food licked off of your body.

Sex Toys

Vibrators

Vibrators can offer a world full of blissful orgasms. They not only help women discover what they need to blast off, but they also help condition our bodies for multiple or simultaneous orgasms. Plus, with their diverse shapes, sizes, colors, and functions, they are fun items to bring into the bedroom when you in an experimental mood. They offer a win-win solution to any relationship-rut problems!

- **The Rabbit**

This vibrator stimulates all the right spots, all at once. Insert the shaft into your vagina and press "play." The device will twirl and stimulate your G-spot, while the pearls at the base of the shaft stimulate the lower vagina. That cute little rabbit attached to the shaft packs a huge punch, too, stimulating your clit with its ears. Choose this vibrator when you're feeling experimental and want to achieve intense orgasms. In other words, this can be your everyday go-to vibrator!

- **The Pocket Rocket**

This is the most discreet of vibrators, looking more like a lipstick tube than a provocative plaything. Apply it directly to your vulva and your clit for some strategic sensual stimulation. You'll be amazed at the amount of zing this teeny-tiny item can generate. Being travel-sized, this vibrator is great for the on-the-go woman, and also is great for stimulating your lover's cock.

- **Hitachi Magic Wand**

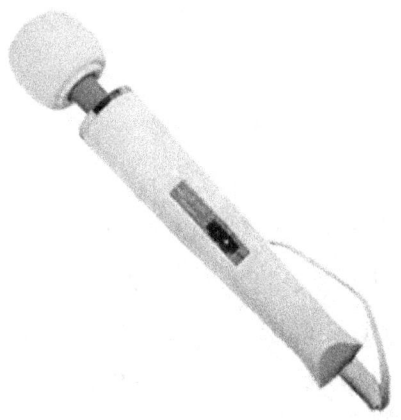

This vibrator is great for massaging your lower back and shoulders—and some other delicious areas. However, it is more powerful than other vibrators mentioned here and can take some time to get used to. It has two speeds and a robust internal motor. If you find it too powerful, fold a washcloth in half and place it over your pubic bone before applying. The real secret to this toy's pleasure is keeping it in slow motion. Move this vibrator across your vulva more slowly than you would normally deem necessary. You want to ensure that every nerve is blasting off, and if you move too quickly, you may not get that effect.

- **Talking-Head Vibrator**

Need some extra-dirty talk when getting down and dirty? This vibrator is your ticket! Made of stunning blue or pink silicone, it has the same pearls at the end of the shaft and ears for clit stimulation that The Rabbit has, and it also has a voice-recorder computer chip that produces CD-quality sound. Record your own (or your lover's) dirty talk, or choose among prerecorded "fantasy chips"— French, Italian, or German lovers, or kinky dominatrix scenarios.

- **The Strap-On Vibrator**

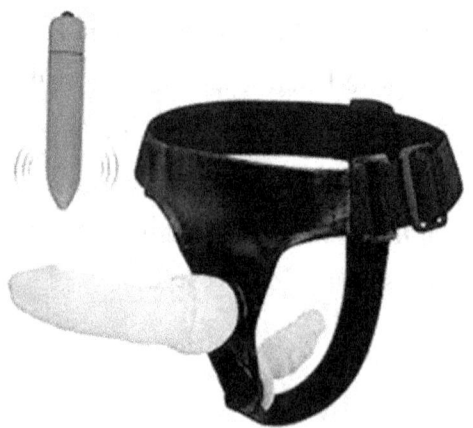

Ever wanted to enjoy the sensations of a vibrator but still have both hands readily available to wander elsewhere? Well, want no more. The Strap-On

Vibrator is a small vibrator that is held in place against your clit with pretty, perfect straps. While it is not as powerful as other vibrators, it is also not as intrusive a toy. Since it's on the smaller side, you can easily introduce it next time you're making love, and he can enjoy the mild vibrations as well.

- **Finger Vibrators**

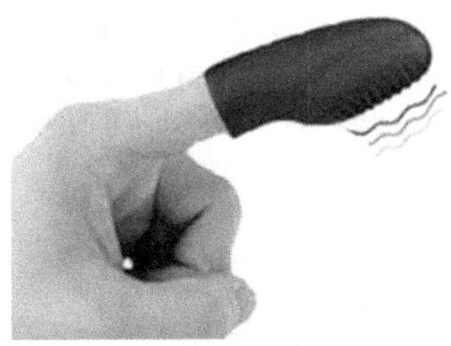

This is a type of vibrator that is small in size and can fit easily on the fingertips. This can be used in foreplay and ideal when used in fingering and hitting the G-spot. Your partner can wear more than one finger vibrator, one vibrator inside your pussy, and one vibrator on the clitoris. That would give the woman an intense orgasm.

Dildos

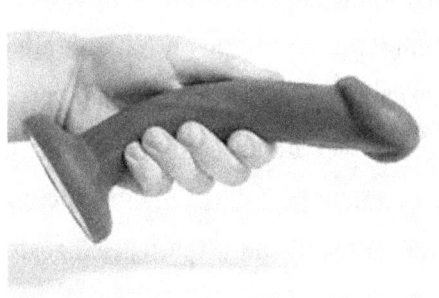

Dildos usually have the same phallic shapes as many vibrators but have no vibrating components. Many women prefer dildos to vibrators because they feel more like the real deal since they are made from lifelike materials like silicone and are the actual sizes of real cocks. Consequently, playing with one actually feels like having real sex. Plus, they come in all shapes, colors, and styles, so you can have fun shopping to find the one that is perfect for you! I suggest using dildos to not only stroke your vulva, labia, and clit as you would with a vibrator, but also for deeper penetration to achieve G-spot stimulation. You can go as gentle, rough, shallow, or deep as you like when indulging yourself with this titillating toy.

- **Strap-On Dildos**

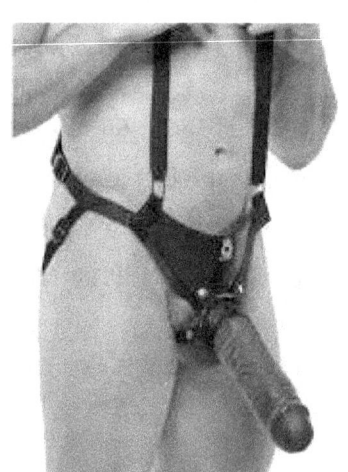

While your lover has a phallic-shaped toy already attached to his delicious body, there are ways a strap-on dildo and a little bit of creativity can maximize your sexual chemistry! Remember, it pays to play well with others! Put a little spin on your traditional sexual roles, and have a naughty "what-was-that?!" experience. Playing with strap-on dildos is perfect for the man who loves anal penetration. He gets to experience the thrill of anal stimulation while you get to take full control of the thrusting and experience a rush of power and lust. Plus, a dildo will stimulate his prostate.

Having a strap-on attached also frees up your hands for other provocative pursuits, like reaching around and playing with his cock as you thrust into his back door.

- **Double Ended Dildo**

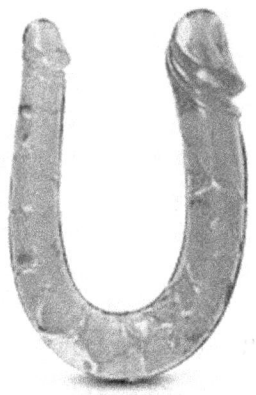

A type of dildo that has no base like any usual dildo would have, it will have two heads at both ends that are used by couples for double penetration at the same time. This dildo is mostly preferred by same-sex couples.

Harnesses

Go strap-on dildo shopping together at a local sex shop or online so you can decide which version of this sex toy will give both your libidos a real boost. Plus, viewing and/or reading about these toys can rev up your engines for some post-shopping nooky! Here are some booty-full basics about the equipment you'll need.

- **Basic Harness**

This has adjustable straps that go around your waist and thighs with a spot to insert a dildo. Its simplicity makes it simply sexy!

- **G-String Harness**

With a lovely leather thong attached to a slim waistband and a single strap running up the center of your butt and over your clit, this strap-on will give your over a large hard-on and give you great stimulation at the same time!

- **The Jock Strap**

This dildo is attached to a waistband that has two straps passing around each thigh. It leaves your vagina exposed so your lover can reach his hands around his back to pleasure you as you give it to him, right!

- **Vibrating Harness**

Oh my! This harness has two little vibrating pads attached, one next to your clit and one where the dildo comes out of the harness for extra anal stimulation. It offers intense his-and-hers happiness!

Other Sex Toys

- **Cock Rings**

Cock Rings are one of the most infamous of male sex toys. Made of rubber, silicone, leather, or metal, they fit snugly around a man's cock and balls. When he's hard, the cock ring prolongs his erection by constricting blood flow to this area and keeping blood in the penis shaft. This means he'll last longer under the sheets, so you're able to blast off several times before he's ready to cum. Not only will you be fully sexually satisfied, but he'll also feel like a regular sex god!

- **Nipple Clamps**

We're not talking about the wooden clothespins of yore, and we mean the newly fashioned fun and stylish clamps that give nipple nerve-endings endless pleasure. For nipple-sensitive men and women, these items are a must-have! Choose the perfect ones for you.

- **Tweezer Clamps**

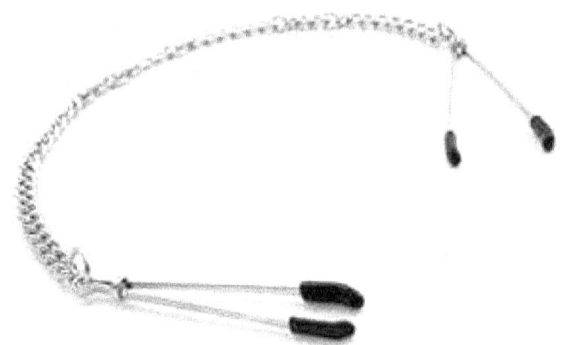

These are the best nipple clamps for novices. They are the most comfortable, and the tension can be adjusted simply by sliding the small ring closer or farther away from the nipple. Also, the narrow, curved, plastic-covered-wire ends close around the base of the nipple, so they leave a tip standing up at attention. This allows easy access for licking and teasing as your or your lover's nipples are squeezed in satisfaction!

- **Clove Clamps**

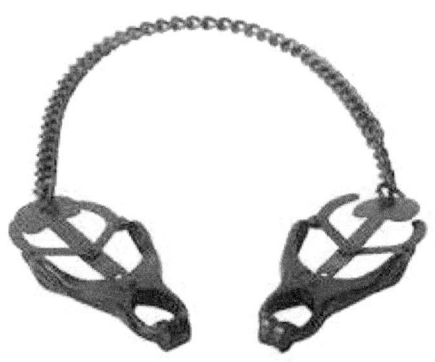

For the more advanced sex-toy player, these nipple clamps are big, sturdy, and slightly intimidating. The pressure is adjustable and is generally hard and rough. The gripper pads consist of mini-rubber disks with stimulating bumps, which also help keep the clamps firmly in place without abrading the skin. Also, there is a chain attached to this nipple toy. The dominant partner can tug on the chain to increase tension and enhance nipple pleasure. Oh, behave!

- **Kitty Clamps**

Again, this is not a beginner's toy. These alligator-type clamps have adjusting screws, limiting how tightly they can be fastened. But here's the kinky kicker—cylindrical weights are attached. Turn the dial and the clamps hum, gently stimulating the captive nipples. Up the dial, and the clamps purr with more passion and make nipples dance with delight!

- **Butt Plugs**

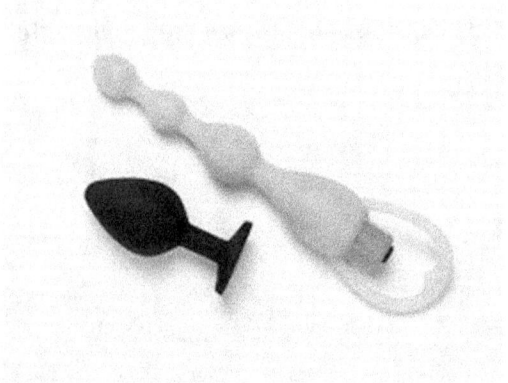

Butt plugs are designed to fit snugly and comfortably into your anus. They are typically cone-shaped, with a flared base that prevents them from slipping into your rectum. You can use them for butt play, to stimulate the endless nerve endings in your anus, or during vaginal sex, to give you the sensation of being filled by your lover, thus making the urge to orgasm that much stronger. An additional plus for him: the bulge in the middle of a buttplug stimulates his prostate.

- **Anal Beads**

Anal beads come in all different colors, sizes, and styles. Like pearls, they are knotted together into place along a string and have a ring at one end. You insert the beads into your or your lover's anus and one by one, pull the beads out. The sensations of the beads going in and coming out of your anus cause your sphincter muscles to contract, which feels incredible and can greatly intensify orgasms in both men and women.

- **Vibrating Panties**

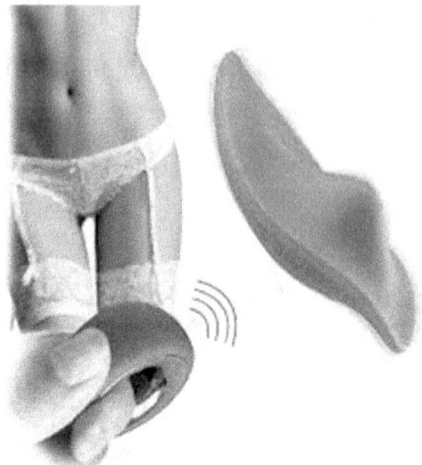

This a type of sex toy that ladies can wear, underwear that has a vibrator attached to it that is controlled by a remote control where one can control the intensity of the vibration. This can be a fun playing activity for you and your partner.

Fantasies

Fantasies can be triggered by your imagination, or by external stimuli, such as an attractive stranger, an erotic picture, a book, or a movie. Whatever tips you off, as long as it's something that gets you off, it's fine to fantasize about it. Fantasies allow you to express your creativity in a sexual way. You may fantasize about things that you want to do but haven't done yet. You can fantasize about things that you did in the past that still turn you on. Or maybe there are some things that you know you'll never want to do, but they're still fun to think about. You can revisit your fantasies as often as you like.

You can feel truly liberated in your fantasies. Masturbation and fantasies often go hand in hand (so to speak), but fantasies also accompany sex for many people. If you are slow to orgasm with your partner, you can call on your favorite sexual fantasy to give your lovemaking a little kick. Fantasies help you focus on the erotic, thus making it easier to reach the point of no return.

If you daydream about how you want to make love, fantasies can give you good ideas, plus they can give you more confidence when you decide you're ready to put your ideas into action. Fantasies are also great for you if you think that you'd like to try a certain sex act, but you're not totally sure. You can experience it in your fantasies to find out if it turns you on before you ever consider acting it out. Sex therapists have discovered that fantasies can be good at helping couples or individuals deal with certain sexual problems. If you put positive, sexually liberating thoughts in your mind, you may become less inhibited about sex. Through fantasy, you can confront your fears about sex and learn to enjoy your sexuality on your own so that you can enjoy it with someone else.

Top 10 Sexual Fantasies

1. Threesomes or Group Sex
2. Sex with a Famous Person
3. Sex with a Friend or Someone You Have a Crush On
4. Sex with a Stranger
5. Sex with Someone of the Same Gender
6. Force Fantasies, Being Tied Up, and Being Spanked
7. Sex While Someone Is Watching
8. Sex in Public
9. Sex in an Exotic Location
10. Sex with a Former Lover

Sharing Your Fantasies

Before you get into deep with fantasies, let's discuss if it's okay to tell your partner your fantasies. You and your partner might decide to talk about your fantasies so you can both learn intimate things about the other. The more you share about your sexual fantasies, the more your partner gets to understand your thoughts on sex. Perhaps your partner never knew you had such a wild imagination, and he or she would love the chance to explore some of your fantasy scenes with you. These are positive reasons to talk about your fantasies. But before you do, you need to keep a few things in mind.

First of all, you should only tell your partner your fantasies if you think he or she can handle hearing them. You must be positive that he or she already understands that sexual fantasies are normal, natural, and won't hurt the relationship. If your partner has a conventional approach to sex, then telling your fantasies could be upsetting to him or her. If you think that your partner would freak out if he or she learned, for example, that once in a while you have same-sex fantasies, then there's no need to tell. It might be interesting to tell a fantasy like that one just so your partner can learn what your imagination holds, but it is never worth telling if you think your partner can't handle knowing. If you want to tell this person, then just be sure that you tell your fantasies carefully. What I mean is, tell your mild fantasies before you disclose your wild fantasies.

Second, if you tell your partner your fantasies, you might want to explain that they are things that you fantasize about while you are masturbating or just things that you daydream about, rather than what you think about while you are having sex with him or her. It is perfectly normal to occasionally think about other things or other people while you have sex with a partner. (That, in fact, even helps keep some people from cheating, because it gives them an outlet to pretend, they are with others.) Yet your partners could get jealous, or even feel threatened if he or she learns that you are fantasizing about someone else while the two of you are having sex.

One last thing and it's essential to remember before you start talking to your partner about your fantasies is to be certain that you tell your partner if your fantasy is things that you don't or do want to act and carry out. Convince your loved one that people do not always want to live out their fantasies! Ensure this is comprehended.

Let's say that you and your partner have talked about your fantasy of having a threesome—two and a man. You think you want to act it out, but you're wavering. You two have a lot of talking to do, and a lot of steps to follow before you decide if you want to go through with it.

If you're thinking about trying to act out any one of your fantasies, there are some things that you should do first:

1. Talk about the positive and negative consequences of your partner. (For example, a negative consequence of a threesome might be jealousy. A positive consequence could be that you have a liberating sexual experience.)
2. While you and your partner are having sex, say a few things out loud—almost as if you're acting out the fantasy—and see how it feels. (Keeping with the example of the threesome, pretend that there is a third person in the room, and role-plays the scene. Pretend you are talking to the imaginary third person.)
3. Get on and watch erotic or porn movies as a couple and look at the kind of sex you're interested in imitating. If what you see in the movie turns you both on, then you are that much closer to realizing that it might work for you. If the movie turns you off, it might not work for you in real life.
4. Talk out the details of what you expect to happen if you act out the fantasy. If both of you can come up with a script, you'll be aware of what will happen, which will make you much more comfortable, confident, and safe of the whole scenario.
5. Ensure one another that when you're acting out these fantasies, you will not continue if one of you dislike what is happening.

6. Talk about it again to be sure you both really want to try it.
7. If you both feel ready, then give it a try when you have the time and opportunity. Good luck! Remember, if you act out a fantasy and you don't like it, you never have to do it again. If this is the case, you can still enjoy it as a fantasy—just stop trying to make it a reality.

But if you enjoyed acting out your fantasy, then you and your partner have added a new and thrilling aspect to your sex life. Some couples find that acting out their sexual fantasies is an integral part of their sex lives, and it gives them the extra excitement that they don't get every day.

Sex Games Beyond the Bed

As you move from games to lovemaking, be creative—don't just opt for the same few positions in bed. If you've got some privacy, explore the rest of your house. The kitchen table is often the perfect height for intercourse. Try the counter for oral sex. Have the woman bend over the arm of the overstuffed chair in the living room for rear entry. The woman can also sit on the arm of the sofa and have her partner kneel on the cushions as he enters her. This is a good position in which to put one of your feet up on the back of the couch. Choose the side of the sofa that will best allow you freedom of movement and maximum G-spot access. The most important point here is that you should feel free to be creative and experiment. Take turns thinking up new places and ways to make love. You've got nothing to lose and a whole lot of fun to gain!

The ancient book of Kama Sutra tells us that good health (physical) and growth (psychological) can happen if we try to do something new out of our usual habits in making love. Always look into nature and find inspiration from it like how certain animals of the opposite sex are always sided by the side. Being out there in nature can give an element of erotic anticipation and mystery to our sex life. You will have more awareness about yourself and your partner when you get yourself to a place or scenario out of your natural environment.

Most of the time, it is hard in the current day to day environments, to get outside that will make you feel safe for doing sexual acts

If you have a backyard with ample privacy, you can modify the area ideal for lovemaking. You can also try doing at your balcony's swing, a sofa in different areas around your home. These things will surely add excitement and new feelings to your sexual life. Try to get inspired by how animals behave when having sex. Try to go to the zoo or watch videos online and see how animals go about it. Old people believe that we can find animals as a source of inspiration in our own lovemaking. Use your nails to scratch lightly and your mouth to bite gently. Use sound to add to the variety. Groan, growl, whimper, howl, hum, and moan!

Naughty Questions

Sometimes, you really do not know what to say. That is the reality you have to face. You can blank on someone. You can overthink too. Do not fret—I got you.

I listed down some suggestions on the questions you could ask or tasks you can do for every game. Consider this an idealist or a cheat sheet. Again, adjust as needed. After all, to make it a better experience for your partner, you cannot adapt to a one-size-fits-all mindset.

A little disclaimer first: the way you phrase and the manner you deliver the statements below can affect how your partner reacts. Read the atmosphere and the person you are with carefully, so you will be able to adjust accordingly.

Some of the questions are based on a psychologist, Arthur Aron's study on intimacy, which was featured in an article in the New York Times called "The 36 Questions that Lead to Love."

They say that if you ask such questions, there is a higher probability of you falling in love because of the level of intimacy it requires to share. I understand the correlation between love and sex. Besides, there is a different sensuality and intimacy involved when you really like a person.

The following are sexy questions and dares or punishments you can use in the games. Feel free to use them according to the route and pace you are going for.

List of Sexy Questions

- Do you prefer to give or to receive?
- What's your biggest turn on?
- Do you prefer lights on or lights off?
- What's the best food to eat to get you in the mood for a hot night?
- What's the kinkiest thing you've done in public?
- When was the last time you had sex?
- What's your wildest sexual fantasy?
- Have you ever imagined being physically intimate with someone inappropriate for you? (E.g. your parent's friend, your friend's ex)
- Who do you think is the best in bed among the group?
- Have you seen anyone in the group naked?

- Do you enjoy long foreplay or you just want to dive right into the action?
- Can you describe your personality in bed in three words?
- Have you ever had a threesome?
- Would you like to be in a threesome or orgy?
- How would you rate the best kiss you've had?
- Describe your first sex in three words.
- Have you ever paid anyone for some action?
- Have you ever masturbated while thinking of a celebrity?
- If you could only have one sex toy forever, what will you choose?
- What porn category do you usually choose?
- Have you had sex with another person other than the person you're currently with?
- Can you tell the story of your most dangerous sex?
- Name one person in the group whom you think has had the most sexual experience.
- Have you experienced anal sex?
- Do you enjoy oral sex?
- Can you name a person you're dying to have sex with but could not?
- Which do you prefer, a single explosive orgasm or multiple orgasms?
- How memorable is your first sexual experience?

- Do you go for one-night-stands?
- Have you had sex in your workplace?

List of Sexy Dares or Punishments

- Reenact the famous "When Harry Met Sally" fake orgasm at the diner scene.
- Make eye contact with the first person who enters the door and run your tongue over your lip suggestively.
- Give a lap dance to a person of your choice.
- Make a body shot on the person of your choice.
- Ask someone in the room to give you a kiss in any part of your head.
- Choose one person/partner to role-play. Pretend you are both strangers in a bar, and try to pick him/her up.
- Stand up still. Your partner can do anything he wants with you for one minute.
- Remove a piece of your clothing.
- Run your fingers all over your body as if you're naked, staying longer on the parts you like to be kissed the most.
- Gesture how you want to be touched in bed.
- Give a person/partner a back hug and stay that way for one round of questioning.
- Close your eyes. Any person who wants to can kiss you for ten seconds.

- Remove your pants for one round of questioning.

- Kneel before one player/partner for one minute.

- Reenact the biggest orgasm you ever had (including the position and the sounds you created).

- Put an ice cube in your top and lie down until it melts entirely.

- Give another player a torrid kiss, with tongue and all, but with a piece of cardboard or paper between your lips.

- Whisper ten foreign words into one player's/your partner's ear seductively.

- Share 5 of your best sexual qualities.

- Take off your undergarment and let another player wear it on his/her head for the remainder of the game.

- Kiss another player on the lips, the number of kisses depending on the number of people you've already slept with.

- Pretend you're modeling for a provocative magazine. Make at least three poses.

- Compliment another player on how you imagine how good he/she is in bed.

- Exchange clothes with someone for the remainder of the game.

- Seven minutes in heaven! The group can choose another member, and the two of you will spend seven minutes together in private.

- Sit beside another player and pretend that you are giving him/her a blowjob/cunnilingus.

- Keep your hands on the thigh of the person on your left for thirty seconds.

- Let another player lick any part of your body.

- Role-play! Choose a player and make him/her blush.

- Share 5 things you like about your partner in bed.

Quick and Easy Foreplay Games for Couples

A few ladies who accept that the way of men's souls through the stomach lose a couple of inches. In all honesty, this is a reality. Ladies who can't recognize food and sex are bad at cooking or in bed. I am not here to hurt anybody's sense of self; however, I will likely share and educate all couples who would prefer not to appreciate the fruitful specialty of adoration. What's more, perhaps on the grounds that the kid or young lady couldn't bear the smell that radiated from our reproductive organs or they thought it was only an obscene thought. To wrap things up; they may imagine that it isn't important at all or that it is an exercise in futility. These three reasons apply to various individuals and couples. In any case, it's not as troublesome as it sounds, yet foreplay is viewed as perhaps the best piece of sex at any point designed by man before at long last having intercourse.

You should initially comprehend that foreplay or oral sex isn't untouchable, as I would like to think I think it is only the start of the state of mind upgrading act to increment sexual excitement before it enters. Let the possibility of sex be the keep going thing at the forefront of your thoughts when having intercourse. Indeed, the delight that originates from foreplay and oral sex is more celestial and more honed than the real demonstration of the entrance. Before I get into the nitty-gritty conversation about foreplay, I'd like you to open your mind and dissipate all legends about it and attempt to acknowledge it as something great. Coming up next are games that you can play with your accomplice before sex

Drive

There is nothing better than accomplishing something somewhat bizarre out in the open or abroad! On the off chance that you need to have a fabulous time outside, Driven Dare is perhaps the best game you can attempt! To play, simply wear some garments, similar to a dark dress for her and a shirt and some delicate shorts for her, and take a walk someplace. Go to elective spots to stop and afterward have the other individual escape the vehicle and accomplish something incorrectly!

Attempt carefully challenging to go to a supermarket to purchase something or cross a timberland region, in the event that you live in the nation. In transit back, put your hand on your accomplice's pony to give him thought of what they need to do together later.

Inquiries Regarding the Path

Have you at any point considered what amount your accomplice thinks explicitly about you? Provided that this is true, this provocative toy makes certain to respond to that consuming inquiry!

To play Strip questions, simply solicit your accomplice an arrangement from provocative inquiries. For each off-base inquiry, you need to remove an outfit!

The harder you pose inquiries, the quicker they will be stripped and afterward, you will think about some troublesome ones like "Where was the hottest spot where we had intercourse?" "What is my preferred mouth position?" and "When was the last time you gave me a climax?" To cause the game considerably more stunning, request that your accomplice shoot and evacuate a piece of clothing for each off-base inquiry!

Commitment or Truth for Grown-Ups

This turn on the great Truth or Dare game is ideal for getting ready for foreplay! Simply alternate inquiring as to whether they need to respond to an inquiry genuinely or dare. This is an extraordinary game to attempt to more readily comprehend your sexual accomplice.

Some great inquiries include: "What is the hottest scene you've at any point found in a film?" 'H "Inform me regarding your most stunning sexual dream." If you decide to set out, make it simple, similar to "I challenge you to give me your hottest striptease now."

Foul Play

Do you think cell phones and sex don't blend? Indeed, it relies upon what you do with them! Filthy Game is a free grown-up just Truth or Dare application that can be altered to suit all degrees of want. Accepting you are on a first date and need to choose "Icebreaker" or relationship mode and need to go straightforwardly to "Foreplay" or "Sex," this application won't baffle you! Simply pick your level and begin having some good times!

Unfairness is ideal for posing inquiries and brave with truth or fearlessness and can assist you with feeling progressively good speaking profanely with your accomplice. At the point when you're all set further, the application additionally covers everything from contacting to infiltrating sex, making it perfect for foreplay, sex, and that's just the beginning!

Drink or Dare

In the event that Truth or Dare is excessively agreeable for your preference, take a stab at playing this variant with too little truth!

Thusly, challenge each other to accomplish something and cause them to decide to set out or have a beverage! You can make the difficulties as provocative or wild as you need; however, attempt to keep them short.

Instances of manageable difficulties include: "Speak profanely to me for three minutes" or "Reveal to me your preferred sexual position," while all the wilder difficulties would resemble "Give me how you like to have a ton of fun." This game is extraordinary for gaining more from one another and investigating your cutoff points, so don't hesitate to utilize the Dirty Game application for all the braver tips!

Monkey See, Monkey Do

On the off chance that you are your accomplice and you feel great watching pornography together, why not play a game with it? To play this game, request that your accomplice pick pornography that truly turns them on. Begin watching it together and request that they pick the best, most sizzling, and most sultry scenes they can discover. The standard is basic; you should attempt to speak to what you see!

In the event that you've at any point watched pornography and needed to attempt it, all things considered, this great sex game could be your opportunity! Now and then places that look great don't interpret well in the room, while on different occasions, attempting what you see can change the manner in which you have intercourse until the end of time! You can't be sure whether you don't attempt!

I Put It in My Mouth

To genuinely build your longing levels, nothing beats the good old blend of sex and food!

To play this game, get stripped, blindfold your accomplice, and have a delectable dinner arranged with a spoon. You needn't bother with a wrap, any tie or scarf will do, and the food can be anything you desire, similar to frozen yogurt, yogurt, or even a lavish pastry!

Since your accomplice is blindfolded, the spoon will wind up in a wide range of spots and there is a straightforward principle: everything that is spilled out to you should lick! Try not to stress; you can control your language in the correct spots!

This is a round of extraordinary certainty and you will adore the vibes that the other half licks your body! Where things go from that point, I leave you...

Extravagant Bowl

To play this hot game, just compose your initial five plans on independent bits of paper, overlay them, and supplement them in a bowl. Cause your accomplice to do likewise. Blend the bits of paper, at that point alternate picking one. Recite the dream so anyone can hear and afterward talk about it.

The Fantasy Bowl game is a non-undermining approach to release dreams that you would some way or another vibe too bashful to even think about exploring. In the event that you need the discourse to make a move, the dreams you offer can generally rouse you!

Profane Pretending Game

Pretending is an incredible method to depict your dreams as you infuse a component of curiosity and energy into your relationship. An incredible method to begin pretending is to watch your preferred show together and calmly ask yourself resoundingly, "Consider the possibility that those two characters are associated?" This can prompt some carefree where you and your accomplice claim to be the characters and speak to the sexual moment they might want to have.

One Moment

This pleasant sex game is ideal for overcoming any issues between getting exposed and beginning foreplay.

Untruth stripped in bed, carry your accomplice to the entryway and pose inquiries about yourself. They can progress for each right answer and should step back for each erroneous answer.

On the off chance that you can hardly wait to have your accomplice above you, pose basic inquiries, for example, "What is my preferred position?" do I lean toward the tongue or fingers? This game is extraordinary for building closeness and expanding enthusiasm levels; when your accomplice reaches you, you will not be able to take your distance!

Bare: Meet You

This game is ideal for making strain before starting foreplay. Rests on the bed and, thusly, run your hands over your accomplice's body, making an effort not to contact them! On the off chance that you get excessively close, your accomplice ought to have the option to feel the glow of your skin. The standard is basic; the individuals who incidentally reach should kiss their accomplice. Keep your score: one point for each kiss!

XXX Denotes the Spot

The standard of this basic foreplay is straightforward: remember a specific point on your body and request that your accomplice kisses each piece of their body until they discover it! This game is stunning for investigating mostly secret erogenous zones like the neck and internal thighs. These joy habitats are regularly forgotten about during foreplay and sex, so this game will assist you with finding your accomplice and EXACTLY know which zones you need them to contact!

Fun Sexy Games for Couples

For level three, the assumption is it has been established that you and your partner are willing to get wild. Consider it as foreplay, if you will. The important thing is both of you are in a private place, and you are more than okay with hitting the sheets. The games below ensure your night is built up to make you thirsty before going all the way.

Strip or Shot

Number of Players

At least two.

Number of Rounds

To be determined by players.

Materials

An empty bottle.

Optional

Booze for shots.

Mechanics

Players will place an empty bottle in between them and spin it—similar to "spin the bottle."

The player who ends up getting the bottle pointed at him/her must choose to strip or shot.

If she chooses to strip, she must remove an article of clothing. If she chooses a shot, she must take a shot.

Repeat steps 1 to 3 until one player is either fully naked or gives up for being tipsy.

Why it's Effective

"Strip or Shot" is pretty much a prelude to the deed. In a nutshell, it's really foreplay to heighten the anticipation prior to sex. A lot of people are into striptease but they do not exactly know how to do it. This game takes care of that aspect. It is striptease under the semblance of a game.

Pro Tip

Gauge how intoxicated you and your partner are. The goal is to be tipsy enough to calm your nerves, but still sober enough to enjoy the night. If you feel like either of you are nearing your limits, by all means, raise the white flag and surrender. There is no need to wait until someone loses all of his/her clothing. As long as you are both ready and excited enough, feel free to end the game under the guise of "I can't take any more shots. I surrender." You're welcome.

Sexy Dice

Number of Players

At least two.

Number of Rounds

To be determined by players.

Materials

A pair of love or sexy dice (available in adult stores or online), or a love or sexy dice app (available online for free)

Optional

Booze for shots, kinky toys.

Mechanics

Players take turns to roll two dices: one has names of body parts, and another has action words.

After Player 1 rolls the dice, she must do the corresponding action to Player 2. For example, dice 1 can have "lips" and dice 2 can have "bite," so she must bite Player 2's lips.

If either player cannot or refuses to do the dare, she must take a shot.

Player 2 will do the same thing from steps 2 to 3.

Repeat until players are heated up.

Why it's Effective

Like "Strip or Shot," "Sexy Dice" gives a teaser of what can happen as the night deepens. It is sensual and sexy, but it does not give away everything. If you are both not yet sure of what to do as foreplay, this is definitely an excellent start to learn how your partner wants to be touched.

Pro Tip

Let the dice help you loosen up. Be mindful of how your partner reacts, what she likes to do, and maybe discover sensitive spots. You can use it to your advantage well along. Alcohol is not a requirement, but if you think you need it to get rid of the jitters and be bolder, feel free to take a shot or two.

A word of caution here: Level three games require you to be responsible. Even if there is alcohol involved, it is very, very, very important to be conscious of your intake. I cannot stress this enough for a number of reasons.

First and foremost, it is for consent. Everything you do with your partner must come from a mutual decision. Second, it is for your pleasure as well. Being wasted does not contribute to your performance. If anything, it just makes it harder for—you get the drift.

Make it a memorable night for you and your partner by only drinking what you can. Tone down on the alcohol and get drunk in physical intimacy instead.

We Can Make It Hotter

You know each other. You want each other. You have hung out with each other's friends. Now, you want to continue going out.

Since you have gone all the way with your partner already, now, you want to do something exciting. Spice things up, as they say. Then, you are in the right place.

Familiarity does not need to equate with boring. If anything, this should help you and your partner become more in sync. Having spent some time together and having the opportunity to "get to know each other" on different levels, you should have a better idea of how you can play with your partner.

Although you have reached level five, you can still play the games from level three, and even some from the other levels. I will be giving you more options for games you can play with your partner in private.

Naked Getting to Know You

Number of Players

Two.

Number of Rounds

To be determined by players.

Materials

None.

Mechanics

All players need to strip down to their underwear.

Each player will take turns hovering his/her hand on his/her partner's body without physical contact.

The partner should feel the heat from your hand.

If a player accidentally or purposely touches the partner, she will be given a punishment.

Why it's Effective:

"Naked Getting to Know You" enables the body to feel a different kind of sensation. It makes you sensitive and makes you yearn for more. Rather than going directly to doing a physical act, the game requires you to take things step by step.

Pro Tip:

Be a tease. Hover your hand on body parts that you know your partner likes getting touched on. Linger on them a little longer than necessary. Your partner will most probably return the favor and tease you back. It might sound like you are at the losing end, but really, think about it deeply. The "revenge teasing" actually stimulates both of you more. By the end of the game, you will find yourself more than ready for some action.

Upgraded Twenty Questions

Number of Players

Two.

Number of Rounds

To be determined by players; ideally, at least ten rounds.

Materials

None.

Mechanics

1. Each player will take turns asking each other a statement which the other must answer. The catch is all questions should be sex-related. This is the R-18 version of the game.
2. A follow-up question is counted as an additional question.
3. Player 1 will ask Player 2 a question.
4. Player 2 must answer honestly. There is no option for punishment or drinking a shot.

5. Player 2 will do the same thing from steps 2 to 4.
6. Saying "Same question" or "How about you?" consecutively is not allowed.
7. Repeat steps 3 to 7 until each person has been asked a total of twenty questions.

Why it's Effective

If the former "Twenty Questions" game seems like tiptoeing on ice, "Upgraded Twenty Questions" legitimizes the sexual questions. Plus, it will entirely be an exchange of inquiries and responses, without pause, without a shot, and without a pass. It will keep you and your partner on your toes. I challenge you to finish the whole twenty questions without getting heated up.

Pro Tip

For this game, it is vital to keep the communication consistent in pacing—pretty much like a rally. Make it seem like a battle of wits. Think that whoever hesitates or groans loses. Not only will your partner get competitive with the exchange, she will also internally curse you for distracting him/her. Be prepared for punishment once you finish the game—if you ever get to finish it.

For level five, in a nutshell, it focuses on keeping things interesting. A word of advice: technology is your best friend. Along with the games written here, a lot of free mobile applications are available for download. Check out some of them when you have time. You could probably find an app or two which suits your taste.

More than playing, do not forget to talk to your partner afterwards too. Maybe she has her own ideas for the following time. Through the games you play, hopefully, you'll be able to open the lines for communication.

Truth or Dare" Hot

If you and your partner like to be naughty when it comes to truth or dares then this is the part for you.

There are three ways to use the information in this.

First, you can use the following requests and questions you can use to supplement your games. In case you run out of things to say or your mind goes blank, you can just flip to this and you have an entire archive of what to say.

Second, you can use this directly to engage in a deeply sexual and arousing conversation.

Finally, if you print this, you can actually cut them out as little cards and drop them into a bowl that you can draw out of well along.

- What, if done right before orgasm, will make it one of the best you've ever had?
- Kiss your way down the front of my neck, down through my crotch, and then back up my spine.
- Perform oral sex on my hand and show me exactly how you like it.
- In what circumstances would you prefer to skip foreplay?
- Would you prefer to be completely silent or incredibly loud during sex?
- What turns you on to see in public?
- Show me how you would try to seduce me into bed for the first time.
- Would you have sex with me in a dressing room or public restroom?
- Go into the room and you have 2 minutes to take 3 sexy photos. Send them to me.
- Where would you most like to have sex that we have not yet?

- Take a picture of us kissing passionately.
- What is your most embarrassing moment during sex?
- Film yourself orgasming for me tomorrow before noon.
- What dirty talk phrase immediately turns you on?
- Tell me about our last sexual encounter in as much detail as possible.
- Do anything you want with me for the following 60 seconds.
- What position or act would you like to do more of?
- Kiss me for 40 seconds.
- What do you like to hear me say during sex?
- Nibble your name onto my back and neck.
- Nibble my ears for 20 seconds each.
- Describe what it's like to have sex with me.
- Put a blindfold on me and run a feather or piece of cloth across my bare chest and thighs.
- Begin touching yourself and continue for the remainder of this game.
- Make your mouth hot with a warm liquid and then give oral.
- Make your mouth cold with ice and then give oral.
- Reenact a random porn scene you find right now by going to Pornhub, typing a random letter, and then choosing the 8th video.
- Download a Kama Sutra app on your phone and find three positions you want to try.
- Eat a banana in the sexiest way possible and keep a straight face.
- Act like a submissive for the 2 minutes.
- Act like a master/dome for the 2 minutes.
- Strip naked and take a walk around the block.
- Groom my pubic region.
- Put Icy Hot or Ben Gay on your nipples.
- Give me a hickey on my ass cheek.

- Pretend to have a VERY loud and intense orgasm.
- Name all the sex toys you have ever used.
- What is the shortest amount of time it can take you to orgasm?
- Drip honey (or chocolate or anything else) onto my chest and lick it off.
- Give me a 3-minute massage.
- If you could receive anything sex-related as a present, what would it be?
- Let's reenact a piece of written erotica right now.
- Would you rather have sex with someone watching, or watch people have sex?
- Which Disney character or cartoon is most sexually attractive to you?
- No underwear for the rest of the day for you.
- Do a cartwheel naked.
- What is your favorite type of porn?
- When did you last masturbate?
- What is the first thing you would do if you could change genders for a day?
- Would you prefer: a partner with a horrible body but great face, or great body and horrible face?
- Switch clothing — whatever fits.
- Show me the most sensitive part of your body.
- What is your sexual brag about your abilities?
- Describe exactly how your orgasms feel.
- What would your stripper theme song be?
- Unwrap a piece of candy in your mouth.
- Both of you will take your bottoms off and start spooning immediately.
- Drip ice water over your partner's naked body.
- Drip candle wax over your partner's naked chest.

- Give five minutes of oral right now.

Never Have I Ever

Number of Players
At least two.

Number of Rounds
To be determined by players; ideally, at least ten rounds.

Materials
Booze for shots.

Mechanics

1. Each player will take turns saying a statement that completes the phrase "Never have I ever."
2. Players may opt to say something they have or never have done.
3. Player 1 will begin by saying "Never have I ever _____."
4. Whoever has made the statement, takes a shot. If you haven't, you don't take a shot.
5. Player 2 will do the same thing from steps 3 to 4.
6. Repeat steps 2 to 5.

Why it's Effective

If the former games are all warm-up activities, this is when it gets a bit hot. "Never Have I Ever," if played right, can become intimate, and not just on an emotional level. It is a chance to know each other's dating and sexual history. Put simply, it is a "no holds barred" kind of game so if there is just two of you hanging out, it is an unspoken agreement to the possibility that you'll be revealing details.

Pro Tip

Despite what I said about the unspoken agreement, give your partner a chance to warm up. Go for simple facts first like "never have I ever had a crush on my teacher" before going for more daring statements. Test the waters by revealing a little of your personal life. If your partner can keep up, you can go two ways: do a push or pull, or make a gradually heated statement.

Push and pull means going for provoking statements, and then alternating them with simple ones. Going the gradual heated statements route is all about building up the tension of making your statement hotter than the last.

Following are some sample "Never have I ever" sentences that you can get ideas from:

- Never have I ever been horny during an office meeting.
- Never have I ever hooked up with someone I met online.
- Never have I ever paid someone for sex.
- Never have I ever been guilty of drunk dialing.
- Never have I ever done it without taking off any piece of clothing.
- Never have I ever been in a threesome or orgy.
- Never have I ever faked an orgasm.
- Never have I ever fantasized about having sex with my best friend's boy/girlfriend.
- Never have I ever seen my parents have sex.
- Never have I ever been rejected by my partner in bed.
- Never have I ever done it in a public place.
- Never have I ever had a one-night-stand.
- Never have I ever done it at the movies.
- Never have I ever role-played with my sexual partner.
- Never have I ever picked up someone in a bar.
- Never have I ever done it inside a moving vehicle.
- Never have I ever done it with my high school teacher.
- Never have I ever swallowed cum.
- Never have I ever given a blowjob/cunnilingus.
- Never have I ever done it in the living room with my parents sleeping in their room.
- Never have I ever done it with a masochist.
- Never have I ever done it with the same sex.
- Never have I ever masturbated for an officemate.

- Never have I ever refused my horny partner in bed.
- Never have I ever sucked/licked my boy/girlfriend while he/she is sleeping.
- Never have I ever done it with a blood relative.
- Never have I ever repeated with someone I had a one-night stand with.
- Never have I ever had sex with someone else in my partner's apartment.
- Never have I ever watched my partner have sex with someone else.

Where to Get Sexy Ideas

You may be reading this as your partner has voiced a fascination in hearing gloomy words in heat of the fire. You may possibly have searched out this publication as you're the person who wants those sweet nothings. Maybe you wish to spice up your sexual life, or you may be simply interested as to the reason your partner wants to talk a lot during intercourse. You may be a wonderful dirty talker that needs a brand-new idea or 2, or perhaps you are simply in the mood to brush upon your own skills that are naughty. No matter the rationale, you've chosen the ideal approach to get the things you require! Discussing filthy has gotten so much part of our sexual culture it has spawned interviews, surveys, forums, and research.

In reality, earlier it had been called "dirty conversation," the craft of saying sexual matters to an enthusiast with all the goal to excite needed a scientific name: lagnolalia. There is a very good reason behind all of this technological interest. Over 80 percent of our sexual life occurs within our minds, meaning fantasy, memory, and appetite are a few of the very effective driving forces behind what we are doing behind closed doors. Various studies have revealed that at the time you actually become physical with your partner, the mind continues to be contributing up to your encounter. Therefore, why don't you select the filthy conversation? This has been at the trunk of mind throughout the day-long anyway!

As stated by Aline P. Zoldbrod, PhD, the author of over just a couple novels on naughtiness, sexy speak to your partner not merely revs play between your sheets, but enhances your own life in ways you never have envisioned. It creates your partner feel great to understand how excited you're, and also your delight makes them feel like the very best fan on the earth. This may explain why cluttered conversation allows you to tingle in all of the ideal places, however, it will not explain the naughtiest dirty conversation may be the hottest. It's one thing to say "fuck" and also find yourself a grin, but it's another to share with your partner exactly the way you wish to fuck them in the most graphic terms it's possible to see right now. The dirtier what, the higher. What is up with this? One term: taboo. By the time we're small kiddies, we're instructed not to say dirty words. Saying naughty matters just isn't exactly what good boys or girls perform. Mentioning that taboo using a partner who makes you feel just like you are breaking the rules, and subsequently causes you to feel adventurous. After the bedroom door shuts behind you and also people's dirty words come from your own mouth, your social conventions disappear. You might seem just angry, and you will possibly get somewhat paranoid and wonder exactly what could occur if anybody, god forbid, discovered you talking like that! You will possibly find flustered rather than have the ability to speak above a whisper. That is when you understand you've only busted down a barrier that you will possibly not have understood was there at the first location. The finest filthy talk pops open a much wider doorway with an extremely crucial question: in case you're able to talk dirty in bed, then everything else would you do? Discussing filthy unlocks doors that you never knew were not there!

Explicit conversation is actually a confidence-booster, too. Not merely does this make him alluring to listen about the situations that you wish regarding him, but in addition, it provides you the pride of focusing on how meticulously you've flipped your spouse. The naughtier you talk, the sexier you're feeling. This sexiness will not disappear once you leave the sack, and also the confidence that you pull out of this spills over into whatever else you're doing. Most of all, talking dirty provides you with the opportunity to voice whatever you actually desire during sex, if with lively speech or dull and to the purpose—in any event it increases your probability of sexual gratification. Zoldbrod highlights that the advantage of foul conversation: it is an established actuality that women who talk in their sexual demands have sex more frequently and therefore are somewhat more joyful. Who doesn't like to check out that?

The Most Significant Part

Before you embark upon the experience of studying how to speak dirty for your partner, maintain the most significant part of sex at heart. No, it isn't the technique during intercourse that one oh my- god movement which produces everybody else you've ever lurked beg for longer. It isn't the dirty conversation—though we'd really like to state this may be by far the main things you can perform during intercourse; it surely does rank a close 2nd. What rankings first? Intimacy. Pure, honest familiarity. There are lots of definitions of familiarity; however, in regards to romantic connections, it boils down to exactly the identical. Intimacy may be your sensation of being near some person which warmth and relaxation that comes from knowing somebody well. It's a lot more than sex—in reality, you can have familiarity without sex in any way. Intimacy is your psychological link and answer you've got to a partner. The latest fall is compared to this cool heat which comes when familiarity is demanded. Becoming confident with your partner, desperate to please, and also prepare to start a part of him may be the secret to an excellent sexual life. But that is only the onset of good stuff. As closeness assembles, our inhibitions drop. The more comfortable you feel with your novelty, the more inclined you should adopt every element of it, although people that you may have formerly considered taboo. In the middle of deep familiarity, the thing that was frightening could be enabling. Talking dirty is much like sharing a secret together with your partner, you which only both of you understand and know. Whenever you are out and around in people, showcasing your best face to the earth, nobody; however, your partner knows just how courageous you are able to definitely be. Whenever you face your colleagues or your supervisor or physician or another person, for instance, they don't have any concept about the genuine person that you feel when you're in bed with your companion. Your partner could be the only person that sees all of the hidden sides of you personally. What a joy, knowing there's something really special that only the both of you talk, no one else may guess! Since you learn how to talk dirty, it opens a completely new universe of potential. You may likely know things about your partner that you won't ever envision, and it is a sure bet he is going to know a little about you! Your openness to talk dirty to him shows him just how much you really would like him and that contributes to improved familiarity between both of you. The closer you are feeling to a partner, the better your sex life will probably be. However, the deepest closeness leaves just a tiny room for shyness, which is where this is useful. Think you are too bashful for filthy conversation? By the time you are finished reading that, you may not be! All these parts are made to take you out of the filthy talk principles towards the talking dirty as a specialist, are certain to definitely get the mind racing, your heart pounding... as well as your own mouth at down and dirty gear.

Dirty Chat Does Not Always Have to Become Filthy

If you listen to the phrase "dirty talk," what's the first reaction? What should you find from the rear of your mind? Odds are once you consider filthy conversation; your initial idea is something which you've seen from a porn picture. It's extraordinary, perhaps somewhat awkward. Maybe it's really "out there" you cannot imagine doing in your bedroom. On the flip side, perhaps it's so dirty it turns you around, and that by itself causes you to feel just a little...well, filthy. You may possibly remember a scene or 2 of a woman talking nonstop from the dirtiest speech she might muster. Maybe even considering this gets you to blush. However, it functions you at precisely the exact same moment. Once you first start to explore dirty-talk, you are entering a place that has ever been thought of taboo. However, open-minded you're, there may be instances when you're feeling somewhat uneasy. However, some would assert that an indication of a very good dirty discussion is the fact that it gets you to squirm in the chair! After all, even in the case, all gender were all comfortable, what is exciting about that? Dirty-talk in that pornography picture may be over-the-top and corny. Nevertheless, the dirty talk become familiar with through this publication won't seem corny at all—it'll seem sexy, complicated, and oh so sexy. To put it differently, do not try to take on this pornography celebrity. They have been reading a script, so being fed up with their traces, and true to life isn't just like that. In actual life, you are able to be more alluring than any pornstar! It requires time to make it happen, but so simply take things slow and focus on the fundamentals. To start with, dirty-talk does not need to be dirty. It is possible to present your joy—and then rev his engine to redline—with all the noises that you create. If you descend in joy, it informs him he is doing something right. If you snore because he enters you, then you are telling him just how much you really enjoy how he believes inside you. How you sigh whenever you close your eyes and cave in the impression could make him feel just like a king. The noises that you create, if groaning or yelling or simply heavy-breathing will let him amounts about the way you're feeling and everything you need him to complete. The design of your voice travels a very long way, too. After you whisper in his ear, then your voice is going to likely be roughened and daunted with the fire you are feeling. That is clearly an all-natural response to one's own body. There isn't one thing bogus about this noise that originates from the mouth, along your fan will recognize it in how the funniest fires unfold. Though candy amorous words and hardcore raunchy kinds have their own place, sometimes simply whispering a word that is sexy can be more powerful than simply belting it out in the middle of passion. Saying just how much you adore the way he rolls you're good, however murmuring it in his ear is much better. Lean small kisses down his torso at the same time you whisper you need to taste him.

Make Love to the Next Level

If you want to try something different but feel like you have been trying many new positions and need something a little different yet, switching up your location can be just the thing you need! Pulling your pants down in a new location can make for a very hot and scandalous encounter. Having sex in a new environment makes things feel new and different and it is exciting for you and your body! Now I'm not saying you need to go full-on public sex here, that will make you scared and unable to perform and not to mention will probably get you arrested. Just a small change in the environment can put your senses on high alert and will make you feel more of everything including pleasure when all of your senses including your touch are heightened.

In the Shower

Shower sex is steamy (literally) and hot (literally) and can make for some very fun body on body action. Make sure the water is the perfect temperature and that you have a mat or something on the floor so you aren't slipping all over the place! Before you start any type of penetration in the water make sure you use lots of waterproof lube because the water in the shower won't be enough of a lubricant for the inside of a vagina and will actually make for some painful friction. Let's avoid that, lube is your friend!

Standing Doggy Style

Standing Doggy Style is a good place to start with shower sex because it will make sure that you don't get sprayed in the face with a hot stream of water while you are trying to focus on having a blissful orgasm. Pleasurable for both parties, Doggy Style in the shower is a new take on an old favorite.

The man stands with his back to the running water with the woman standing in front of him, facing away from him. The woman then bends forward and can put her hands on the edge of the tub or the wall of the shower for support. The man slides his penis into her from behind, grabbing onto her hips for a deeper thrust and then they are ready to go for it. This position has a good chance of the man being able to hit the woman's G-spot with his penis so that this position will be greatly enjoyed by the woman. The warmth and the wet environment of the shower are sure to make for an unforgettable sexual encounter.

Kneeling Shower Sex

If you both are in the mood for a position that doesn't need you to focus too much on difficult positioning and holding yourselves up in a slippery shower, you can try the kneeling position. Have you kneeled on the floor of the shower, one person behind the other? From here you can go in many different ways.

You can use this position as foreplay as you both reach around to pleasure the other's genitals with your hands before you move to the bedroom together. You can also use this as foreplay before switching to another position for penetration in the shower. Or you can start penetration right away. For penetration, you will have to adjust each of your heights on your knees to line up your erection and her vagina to meet nicely for smooth penetration. This position is full of possibilities and is a very hot way to get you both in the mood for whatever is to come either in the shower or out of it.

In the Car

Car sex is an old favorite, hailing from the days when we lived with our parents and had to find other places to get dirty than the single bed surrounded by posters of popstars. We couldn't risk being found out! Why not go back to those days where you were nervous and doe-eyed for a close encounter in the back seat of your car? Or if you lust after each other so strongly that you cannot wait to get home, pull over and rip each other's clothes off to have a car session right then and there! Having sex in the car get the windows all steamy and the temperature rising. This hot little car has you all over each other, grinding on those old car seat cushions to the tune of the radio.

The Side Saddle

Sometimes, the positions that seem to be basic when you are at home and in bed may be that much more exciting when you are in a new environment, especially in a confined space. The Side Saddle is one of these positions.

The man sits in the back seat facing forward, the way you would normally sit in a driving car. The woman then sits on his lap across the back seat, facing the side window with her legs stretched across the back seats. The man now puts his penis inside the woman's vagina from here and can either thrust his hips up and down into her, or lift her up and down on his penis. This makes for great use of the confined space of the back seat, giving both people enough room but is still confined enough to feel sexy and close. This position can be done discreetly and that makes it even sexier. Try imagining that you are in the back of a cab on your way home from the bar with a hot person you met that night. You are making out and are both so horny, itching to get into each other's pants and you simply can't wait any longer. The girl opens the buttons of your pants, lifts up her dress, slides onto your lap and you begin to have sex right then and there without the cab driver being any the wiser. You have to be as quiet as possible, stifling the moans of pleasure because you don't want him to find out what is going on in the back seat.

The Lap Dance

The Lap Dance is a more classic position but is just as hot as any other. This position doesn't need much setting up because at this point you would probably already be in the midst of a steamy car make out in this exact position. When you want to quickly transition from an innocent front seat make out to a full-blown hump session, this one is the quickest way to get down and dirty.

This position is done with the woman on top of the man as if she is giving him a lap dance, which is where it got its name. She is on his lap facing him with her legs on either side of his hips. You can even do this position with most of your clothes still on, to bring that element of urgency to your session and turn you on even more. The woman can take the man's penis out of his pants just enough to get access to it, slide her panties to the side, and lower her down onto his erection. From here, they are ready to go! They should be careful that she doesn't hit her head on the roof when she starts to get so into the mood that she is thrusting herself up and down with vigor. For another element of turn-on and closeness, the man can even hold onto the woman's head to protect this from happening. With his free hand, he can slide his fingers up her shirt and stimulate her nipples, or he can grab onto her butt cheeks. This position doesn't necessarily require penetration, so it is good for any combination of genders and genitals, it is just as easy to take each other's pants off before getting into the position and begin fingering each other or giving a hand job. Creativity is your friend in car sex!

In Public

Public sex is risky and you have to be sure that nobody else is around that will be scarred and greatly offended, but if not, it can be very exciting. Knowing that you are being naughty and rebellious is sure to ignite a fear-driven horniness deep within. The thrill of being outdoors or in public anywhere can make you feel free and uninhibited. Sharing this moment with the other person is sure to make you both giddy with a little healthy dose of the scariest. Outdoor sex and public sex can be two very different things, although outdoor sex usually comes with the chance that someone might see you.

Swimming Sex

This leads me to swimming sex. Both outdoor and public, this one can be risky but very exciting if you do it the right way. Try having sex in the water, whether in a pool, in a lake, in the ocean, or in the hot tub. Water sex can be the places to try those tricky positions you want to try but maybe aren't strong or flexible enough to do on land. In the water, you are both virtually weightless and the water lets your joints move into positions they wouldn't be able to with all of that gravity here on earth. Because you are both so light, you can hold each other up or move each other around in ways you aren't normally able to.

Tree Hugger

The man is standing in water deep enough to cover his waist, preferably somewhere around the depth of his ribs or chest. The woman stands in front of him, facing him, and then climbs into his arms, wrapping her legs around his waist and her arms around his neck. He will hold her up by her butt cheeks. Then, he can put his erection inside of her and do the thrusting with his arms by lifting her up and down on his penis.

This position is difficult to do on land, but in the water, you will be able to do it with ease. Being submerged so that you have just enough privacy will make you feel exposed enough to get turned on, but not too exposed so that you cannot concentrate on your pleasure. Your genitals will be safely hidden under the water and nobody will be able to see them unless you are in a crystal-clear sea (in which case you'll be like a fish in a fishbowl)! Her boobs can be hidden by a bikini, unless this is a nude beach or you are skinny dipping at night, and then she could have her boobs pressed against your chest while you hold her. Talk about romance. Relax into the flotation that the water provides for your bodies and feel the pleasure that the other person is providing for you. Look at each other in the eyes or have a steamy make-out session while nobody knows what is really going on under the surface. For an added turn-on factor, you will have to be quiet and stifle your moans when you are close to orgasming so that nobody catches onto what is happening. Trying to keep quiet in intense pleasure only makes you hornier.

Tips to Spice up Your Love Life

Investing time in learning the teachings of the Kama Sutra can help you provide mind-blowing orgasms to your partner. It can be very difficult for some people to reach orgasm but when you have the skills you need it can be achieved quite easily. There are some major components to ensuring that somebody can reach orgasm. In terms of a woman, they need to be extremely comfortable in their situation should be able to climax. Men are a little bit easier when it comes to this area; however, sometimes it can be difficult for them as well.

Obviously, the tips and tricks that you will use to ensure your lady has a mind-blowing orgasm are going to be quite different than the ones to ensure that the male counterpart is getting his. There are different tactics that are going to be used in different situations. It does not have to be difficult to ensure that your partner reaches orgasm as long as you have the information and ability to do it. Let's take a look at both sexes and what you can do to ensure that they have mind-blowing orgasm's each and every time you participate in a sexual encounter.

We're going to start off by looking at the ladies. There are a variety of different things you can do to make it easier for her to achieve an orgasm. Most women admit that they have faked a few orgasms in their life. Unfortunately, a few is a gross understatement for how many times most women have faked it. It is unfortunate that they believe that they need to do this to make their sexual partners feel satisfied. Men, you must remember that you can't pressure a woman into having an orgasm. It is something that is going to take time and honestly, there are going to be times she absolutely cannot get there. This is OK as the experience of sexual intimacy is fulfilling enough during those times that orgasm cannot be achieved.

The environment that you put your lady and will play a big role as to whether or not she is going to be able to climax. As noted, women need to feel comfortable and relaxed to be able to have an orgasm. So, setting the mood for your woman is more important than ever if you want to ensure that she has an orgasm every time you enter into sexual intercourse.

We cannot iterate enough how important taking your time and investing it in 4 play is. This tactic will help to get her warm before actual intercourse begins. It takes time for a lady to become truly aroused and foreplay will guarantee that she is. Using your mouth in your hands you can stimulate all of her erogenous zones and have her reeling when it's time actually to penetrate her.

You need to keep in mind that for most women it can take an average of about 20 minutes for them to achieve climax. So, when a man ejaculates prior to this it can be very frustrating for the woman. If you cannot last longer to provide her with the time, she needs to climax don't leave her stranded. You can pleasure her after you have reached orgasm to ensure that she also gets hers. It can be a little bit messy, but she will certainly appreciate it if you decide to slide in a couple of fingers to finish her off after you have climaxed.

Another great tip for ensuring that your lady reaches orgasm is to focus on her clitoris. Most women cannot achieve orgasm from simple penetration. The combination of penetration and clitoral stimulation is utterly amazing from the female's perspective. In fact, most women would rather you simply focus on their clitoris to help them achieve climax. Penetration is fantastic and most women enjoy it; however, it is likely not going to be enough to get her there truly.

You also want to make sure to encourage dirty talk. Being naughty before and during intercourse can be truly stimulating. It turns women on and allows them to relax. Most women do not want to participate in a sexual encounter with an extremely shy man. So, be bold and open your mouth to state all of your wants and desires. She will truly appreciate it.

Last but not least, work on finding her G-spot. Yes, the G-spot actually exists. It is typically located a couple of inches inside of her vagina on the front wall. With a little bit of pressure and a circular pattern of movement, you can stimulate her G-spot. This can lead to female ejaculation and some of the best orgasms she has ever experienced in her life. If you add to that some clitoral stimulation you will seriously be driving her wild.

Now that we've looked at a few things that men can do to ensure that their ladies have amazing orgasm's let's reverse the role. Figuring out exactly what to do to ensure that he has a mind-blowing orgasm can seem intimidating for some people. This is especially true if you are lacking in, experience. Keep in mind that sex is a learning process and you will get better the more that you do it. In addition, the more you know your partner is the better level of communication you have the easier it will be to do the things that truly please them.

While it may be easier to give your man an orgasm than it is for him to give you one you need to realize that there are definitely different levels. Some orgasms for men are simply OK while others are completely off the charts. Obviously, we want to provide our male counterparts with orgasm's that are consistently off the charts. Let's look at some different techniques that can help you accomplish this.

Just like women, men need to be relaxed and undistracted to achieve orgasm. So, setting the mood can be advantageous in helping them push their daily stresses out of their minds and focus on the intimacy that is about to commence. In addition, foreplay is almost as important to men as it is to women. This ramp-up. It allows the sexual tension to heighten and make intercourse much more stimulating.

When intimacy is done right both partners are focused on each other. Oftentimes, this leads to a man pushing off his orgasm until his female counterpart has been satisfied. One way to ensure that your man has a mind-blowing orgasm is to tell him he doesn't need to worry about you. Make the sexual session all about him. Allow him to lay back while you take control. Encourage him to climax whenever he can even if it is quickly. This can be very freeing for a partner and reduced their level of worry which, in turn, will allow them to have a mind-blowing orgasm.

Another great piece of advice that can help your man have a mind-blowing orgasm is to withhold it for a few days. Yes, this can be difficult for both parties. It is especially true if you have an exceptionally sexual relationship. By denying actual intercourse you can really ramp both parties up to have seriously intense orgasms. It will take a bit of willpower; however, you will both be appreciative in the end.

One other tip that can help your man achieve a mind-blowing orgasm is to surprise him. In the afternoon quickie is not something most women initiate. However, it is something that should be initiated more frequently. Surprising him with a random tumble in the sheets it can really heighten his level of pleasure and the experience he has during intercourse.

As with all things, the tips that we have given you to help heighten the level of orgasm for your partner are only a few of the many things that work. If you have tried all of these things continue to do some research as there are more options out there. Simply trying to ensure that your partner is achieving excellent orgasms is a step in the right direction and the more you try the more successful you will be.

5 Tips to Increase Intimacy

It is part of the reality that the connection between two people will decrease over the years, even though they began their relationship with a great level of passion and excellent sex life, though this can be a norm and, for some not considered a priority, a sexual spark in a relationship is truthfully an essential ingredient for a fulfilling and happy life with your chosen special someone.

If you observed and felt that the sexual spark both of you used to have is now fading, it may be giving you some anxious thoughts about what the future has in store for your relationship. Are you may be asking if that connection can still come back, and if it won't, what would happen to the relationship?

Several studies and cases with shreds of evidence on relationships and sex answers this question with a yes, that it is with a high possibility that you can come up with ways on how to rekindle and increase your connection with your partner, in all aspects including sex. For you to understand it better, we must familiarize ourselves with the best techniques you can utilize and how these can help you. Not only will these techniques help you revive physical intimacy with your partner but can also help in fostering meaningful, healthy emotional and mental health.

To start, we will look at the different stages of intimacy so you'll be able to know where you stand and what you will go through as you address the issue.

The Stages of Intimacy

Being Infatuated: Basically, what people fondly call as the honeymoon phase where both of you are somewhat obsessed with each other. You are so elated and so in love and can't get enough of each other.

The Landing Stage

In this stage, you now see your loved one as a real human being who is imperfect and has flaws. It's one step down a pedestal, and adjustments on sharing life with them are being made.

Burying Stage

The stage where your energy is focused outside of your relationship (less time for your partner; rather, you are focused more on organizing, planning, fixing things for your gain

Rejuvenating

Now, you have a change of heart, and your focus comes back to the relationship, and you start to become aware of how attractive your loved one and all those flaws make him/her imperfectly perfect for you.

Love That Lasts

This stage usually occurs in the fifth year of your relationship, and this is where the feeling of happiness, stability, support, love, and security is felt by both parties.

Five Intimacy Techniques for Couples

Seeking the help of a counselor or sex therapist can be a good and positive step, you can take if you are struggling with your sex life. Through their expertise, it is good to help you remove your old, bad, and unproductive methods of interacting.

For some who may find this step a little bit complicated and too tedious, you can do the following intimacy exercises to help you in increasing your physical, emotional, and mental intimacy in your relationship. Go over them and apply all that seems helpful for you.

1. Respiratory Connection Exercise

Stressful and hectic schedule in life is the main reasons why intimacy in a relationship decline.

Knowing this, you must find ways on how to relax in order to increase your connection. You must encourage your partner to relax with you like listening to or watching about mindfulness is a great way to ignite something between the two of you.

Afterward, do this breathing exercise, which involves you sitting in front of your loved one and resting your forehead against them. Now, your eyes must be closed and take in deep breaths and slowly release it. With this, you'll find yourself getting more relaxed, free, and lighter.

For both of you, doing this will give you the feeling of having more connection and good synchronicity because you are aligned physically, and both of you created a rhythm. This will then lead to a deeper connection like hugging and kissing, etc.

2. View of The Soul

Both on emotional intimacy and sexual intimacy, the Soul Gaze exercise focuses surprisingly on the power to look into another person's eyes. Again, this technique helps slow your mind and focus your energy on your partner.

Experts recommend doing this at least a few times a week. It only takes a few minutes (maximum five), but it can have a profound impact on how you feel about each other.

To perform the Soul Gaze exercise, just sit in front of your partner and look him in the eye. Think of the adage that the eyes are a "window to the soul" and see what you are collecting from your lover.

What do you feel, remember, or desire? What do you think they are experiencing?

Don't worry if you're a little uncomfortable with this at first; trust that it will be easier and more relaxing and intimate.

3. Give Tenderness for 15 Minutes

In reality, it will not happen overnight; you can't reproduce a sexual connection right away, yet you can methodically create habits and routines that amplify your odds of connecting with them at all levels. The method of the 15-minute sensitivity practice is that it will assist you with feeling increasingly comfortable being touched by your loved one. These encounters can get tense and on edge if your sex life is not that good.

Choose an area or space for the two of you then sit together, glancing in one direction. For instance, you can be close to one another, or you can stay behind your partner's seat. In this manner, a sort of delicate and fragile touch starts. It isn't unexpected to do this activity, concentrating on brushing the couple's hair/kneading the scalp or even giving a massage.

You can explore different avenues regarding various methodologies and see which ones work best and satisfies you. Make these habits for the both of you or maybe even just for you when your partner is not available

4. Uninterrupted listening

You may not imagine that listening has a lot to do with the sexual connection with a partner.

In any case, when you don't feel explicitly close, it regularly has a great deal to do with feeling unvalued, and we feel that nobody is tuning in to us to listen. Once more, this technique or exercise will only be under 15 minutes for each individual. It can truly make you connected as one team again.

To begin with, set a clock for ten minutes. In this set of minutes, let your partner voice out everything and anything he/she desires to tell you, maybe it be negative or positive. Listen cautiously, truly tolerating it, and don't make any interruption

After, when he/she is finished talking, think about what you have heard by repeating it and reflecting on your partner's primary concerns. You will be stunned at how significant and understanding it tends to be! At that point, reconfigure the clock and take the chance also to express yourself before your partner.

5. Sensuality and Consciousness

At the point when you wonder how to recover connection and intimacy in your marriage, you may accept that if it does not happen spontaneously, then it is not genuine. This tantric practice called Conscious sensuality can do something amazing for physical closeness and intimacy.

They start by taking five minutes to look at one another without flinching and inhaling deeply. At that point, go through five minutes stroking and touching your partner's torso, neck, and face before letting them do likewise with you for an additional five minutes.

Simply center around how it feels without essentially attempting to advance towards openly sexual actions. You can likewise try it if you like; however, you can likewise consent to limit this technique to kisses until you are not, at this point, agreeable.

Online Interactive Sex Games

Our technology today not only helps us simplify and make our lives convenient but also to make it exciting and fun. Games have been one aspect of technology that grew in terms of new graphic and animation features and pretty much attracted lots of people and players online. It's the same with how games involving sex has evolved. Going online, you'll see a lot of different online games of such nature.

In these themed online sex game platforms, usually, you control a computer-generated character that can be of a different race, look, and sexual orientation.

Apart from that, there are available different levels of interaction with other users you should achieve.

Your characters online can be customized according to what appearance, dress, and characteristics you like them to have. The player can also control the different activities it can participate in and what conversations the avatar can hold. For some, these sex games online can be a way for them to interact with real people, freely and with less hesitation. Interacting with real people can happen through chat, microphone, or even webcams.

Though this can't be at par with real interaction, people use these platforms to meet new people they can hang out with or sometimes to compensate for temporary periods of loneliness. For some who are not that good with people face to face, this can be a way for them to boost their confidence and have that feeling of control. In the case of other people, using these online sex game platforms can be used to ignite and revive an active sex life. This is ideal for those couples who are in a long-distance relationship. Some popular online sex games are found on many websites such as porngames.com, interactivesex.com, playsexgames.com, and so much more. You can use any search engine you have and search for online sex games, and a lot of results will be yielded.

If you're not keen on using online sex game platforms, you can resort to some erotic apps to install on your smartphone. For example, there is Planet Porn, a wide selection of videos and free images to whet your imagination. At the same time, for couples' sex games, you can choose between Ultimate Sex Games for Couples for iPhone and The Foreplay Game for Android. If you want to try tantric sex instead, there is Tantric Sex Deck. The important thing is that the apps are helpful for experimenting. The phone must not become an annoying third party! Unless you decide to use it for sexting: if a couple is forced to stay away, they can still carve out a spicy moment. In fact, at a distance, you can exchange sexy images, perhaps through an app that does not leave a mark like Snapchat, and messages with high erotic content. The only precaution is always to be attentive to privacy, and to do sexting only with a person you trust, to avoid unpleasant inconveniences such as the diffusion of photos and screenshots of the chats.

Conclusion

Sex games for couples can be a useful way to have a pleasurable erotic experience. It is best to make yourself familiar with the particular sex game that you want to try. Then, get a lube that is compatible with the sex game and you will have a fantastic orgasm that you'll remember for a lifetime.

Sex games spice up the relationship of couples and it gives a new feeling of pleasure, love, and friendship within couples. So, try to play sex games within your relationship and enjoy life to the fullest.

Some couples feel that sex games are childish but the reality is that If couples enjoy by playing sex games with each other then it becomes very natural in both the partner to change their mindset and start enjoying the whole thing.

With a partner, you can spend some good time while playing sex games with them and you can spend some memorable time with them.

However, to play sex games I think it is best to check the environment and it should not have any disturbance like phone calls from friends, some disturbance from your neighbor, or the hustle and bustle of the city life. That will make your mood down.

For couples with kids, sex games activities should be done in private as it could affect the mind of kids to have sex before marriage.

Play sex games with your partner in private and make your relationship stronger because sex is the power of a relationship that keeps the relationship strong.

Sex games range from different things like strip poker, striptease, lap dance, porn movies, etc. Therefore, if you want to try some new things then play sex games with your partner and make your life happy.

Sex games and role-playing with your loved one is possible through phone sex also because Phone sex is one of the most passionate enjoyable experience that brings you together with your partner.

Simply put sex games is an enjoyable game, which helps the partners to increase their love, friendship, strength, and closeness to each other.

In addition, to make it more exciting, you can enhance your part by adding sex toys to the game. Here are some exciting and useful toys which you can use while playing sex games:

One of the toys that can help you to fulfill your erotic desire and make you feel more sexually eager is the vibrator. The vibrator is a device that has the function of vibration and you can use it to arouse yourself and to arouse your lover.

Sex toys are in different products like for anal, for female and for male. Vibrators also have different tastes, shapes, and functions.

Now a day both men and women can use sex toys and vibrators. Toys are safe to use in sex games.

So if you are an individual who is interested in having sex with your partner with the help of sex toys than you should definitely use sex toys.

However, the most important thing in sex games is the trust between you and your partner. If you both are confident about the game sex then the game will end up with a wonderful ending.

www.ingramcontent.com/pod-product-compliance
Lightning Source LLC
Chambersburg PA
CBHW070107120526
44588CB00032B/1370